The Road to Silence

By the same author:

Poetry
Against the Storm
The Sheltered Nest

Memoir
In My Father's House

Editor
Poets of Munster
An Introduction to Irish Poetry
The Cork Anthology

The Road to Silence

an Irish spiritual odyssey

Seán Dunne

New Island Books / Dublin

The Road to Silence
is first published in 1994 by
New Island Books,
2, Brookside,
Dundrum Road,
Dublin 14
Ireland

ISBN 1 874597 12 X

New Island Books receives financial assistance from
The Arts Council (An Chomhairle Ealaíon),
Dublin, Ireland.

Cover design by Jon Berkeley
Cover photograph courtesy of The Cork Examiner
Typeset by Graphic Resources.
Printed in Ireland by Colour Books, Ltd.

Our real journey in life is interior.

Thomas Merton

for Trish Edelstein

1

As a child, I saw the world with a religious dimension that I have never lost. At its most negative, this consisted of a morbid fear that punishment would ensue if I broke the rules of Catholicism. There were times when I felt that a dreadful punishment would follow not merely if, say, I murdered someone, but even if I stole an apple from a classmate's schoolbag.

I desired to do good, but not because I saw this as worthwhile in itself. Rather, I feared that I might come to harm if I did otherwise. The threat of Hell lay behind every sinful action and affected me with such force that it can still haunt my mind. Even now, I am still not sure that the motives behind some of my actions and attitudes are free of this morbid fear, albeit in another form.

When I reached adolescence, I found that my childhood beliefs could no longer sustain me. The result was, at various times, an agnostic uncertainty, a void and, even, a mere going-through-the-motions of religious observance. Yet while I felt unable to practice the form of religion with which I was familiar, I was still left with a strong sense of spirituality. I found it impossible to believe in nothing or to believe that the world around me was a kind of cosmic fluke in which myself and others were merely accidents. I sensed the existence of another dimension and hovered between honest doubt and utter confusion. My beliefs up to then had more to do with convention than with conviction and my disinterest in convention led me to reject them. At its worst, as Carl Jung learned from many of his patients, this gap between religious certainty in childhood and spiritual floundering in adulthood could lead to break-down. To some extent, this is what happened.

In my childhood, every situation was permeated with rules and the main aim seemed to be to act in such a way that one would not be damned as a consequence of one's actions. Catholicism was a dark and powerful father whose shins I would eventually kick. At times, like some Greek parricide, I felt an urge to kill and expunge it, even as I felt, perversely, that it would punish me for doing so. Strangely, for a faith in which Mary is so dominant and in which so many of those saints and mystics who mean much to me now are mainly women, the Catholicism of my boyhood seemed to have very little of the feminine about it. It appeared to be a world of threats and strictures, of regulations and warnings, force and punishments — in short, a world driven by the worst aspects of the masculine element.

I realise now that much of my intense involvement with religion as a child was connected with my mother, a devout woman who died when I was four and whose death became a wound that shaped me as a person and as a writer. I found her rosary beads in a worn leather pouch. Her wedding missal lay among old clothes in a drawer. A prayer-book, which she had owned in girlhood, surfaced among wallets of photographs. When, as a teenager, I ceased to practise as a Catholic, a part of me felt that I was acting in a way that would have disappointed her deeply. I felt an abundance of that famous Catholic guilt to which so many non-Catholics point as a negative inheritance. In a world where certainty is regarded as preferable to doubt, I suppose it should embarrass me now to admit such things. Guilt is a sign of uncertainty and is sometimes seen as a form of immaturity or as a retardation of the spirit. At its healthiest, guilt is the mark of an active conscience but, taken too far, it can also be a sign of spiritual sickness. Such an attitude must seem pathetic to some whose frame of mind is far healthier and whose childhoods were free, for example, of the fear that would grip me lest my teeth touch the communion wafer as it melted in my mouth.

Old fishermen, like my grandfather, talked about a fish called a John Dory which has an obvious mark on its skin. It looks roughly like a thumb-print. The fishermen believed it was the mark of Christ's thumb. It marked this fish ever since Christ ate a John Dory at the Last Supper, just as a cross marked the backs of donkeys since the day Christ rode into Jerusalem. Oddly, another culture also saw this fish as touched by deity; the Latin name for a John Dory is *Zeus Faber* — Zeus the maker. Catholicism left a mark on me just as its founder is said to have left his mark on this fish.

Yet there were many times in my childhood when religion touched me in a different way, which was free of fear. It was lyrical, and it shot the everyday through with a sense of the otherworldly. Such occasions had a sense of innocent excitement and ceremony without scrupulosity. The annual Corpus Christi procession was one such instance. Then, religion ceased to be something that was centred in fear and it came into the street like a released kite. It was a day I loved.

On the feast of Corpus Christi, small altars were set up in the front windows of houses in the streets of Saint John's Park, our small suburb of local authority houses in Waterford. In our house, the altar was made by setting chairs atop the sitting-room table and then draping a white sheet over them. Jam-jars were scrubbed clean and boiling water was poured over the labels, which were then peeled away. The jars were filled with small flowers from the back garden (I remember including dandelions and buttercups in this crude bouquet) and were placed on the sheet.

For as long as I could remember, a picture of the Sacred Heart was set over the mantelpiece in the kitchen. It was taken down and dusted. Then, with its chord hanging loosely behind it, it was set between the jam-jars.

It leaned against the chair that stood on the table. Anyone looking in from the street would have seen neither table nor chair but simply the picture set against the vivid sheet, flanked on each side by a jar of flowers.

Many of the sitting-room windows in the street had the same scene with minor variations: a glass vase instead of jam-jars; a small statue of the Infant of Prague instead of a picture; a plastic statue of the Virgin Mary which someone had bought when on the Waterford and Lismore diocesan pilgrimage to Lourdes. These plastic statues were really bottles, and the small blue crowns on top could be unscrewed. The bottles contained Lourdes water which was said to be a remedy for sickness and an agent of miracles.

The procession and the construction of the little altar became a kind of street theatre, and I got from it the same excitement that came from making small theatres out of shoeboxes, or from assembling scrapbooks. I became engrossed in the process.

It was on Corpus Christi that children made their First Communion. The young girls joined the procession, attired like miniature brides in white dresses and veils. Some wore white gloves as well, or carried prayer-books dangling from white or gold cords around their wrists. Boys walked in the procession too. I walked among them when I was seven, wearing my new school blazer with a rosette pinned to the lapel. When I grew older, I saw rosettes pinned to horses and riders who had been victorious in show-jumping events. Since I had never seen rosettes used for any purpose other than First Communion, this seemed startling and even sacrilegious. A medal was pinned to each boy's rosette. Sometimes a small, plastic chalice was glued to the rosette's centre. I loved to whisper the word *rosette* to myself; like the words *myrrh* and *benediction*, it had an aura of holiness. Such words encompassed mystery within their sounds.

There were stories which had this aura as well. It was said, for example, that no one should speak to a priest carrying the communion host to a sick person, as if even the utterance of a word would sully the sacredness of his journey. Another dictum declared that a secret told in confession could never be revealed, and that priests had been put to death because they refused to break this sacred seal.

The priest, wearing elaborate vestments with hems that gleamed with a golden edge, walked at the head of the procession and carried a gold monstrance. A wide, white host was fixed behind glass at its centre and lines spread from this core like the rays of the sun. The priest walked beneath a canopy that was supported at each corner by men carrying wooden poles. Gold tassels hung from its sides and once, when I went close before the procession started, I ran my hand against them and felt them swish softly through my fingers. The priest's round face looked uncomfortable in the heat. He was famous for his ability to raise funds through the organisation of bingo sessions. The calling out of numbers from coloured balls seemed a long way from his appearance on Corpus Christi, when he moved through the streets with a congregation walking behind him as prayers were said aloud or hymns were sung:

O sacrament most holy,
O sacrament divine...,

I loved the sight and sound of such an exotic procession through our streets which suddenly lost their considerable drabness. It would match any similar event in Italy or Spain. The memory of it recurs when I see Mafia movies in which such processions sometimes feature. While the movie shows a corpse in a room overlooking the procession, or uses the accompanying music of a brass band to drown out a gunshot, the processions in my childhood were drama enough in themselves. Afterwards, the white sheets were taken down, the picture was put back on the kitchen wall, and I walked across the trampled grass that grew in a wide space at the heart of the estate where crowds had knelt as the priest raised the host and a small set of bells tinkled. On other evenings, the main sight in the street was of men coming home from work or of children playing on footpaths. The sight of the procession transformed everything and, for me, gave the streets the atmosphere of an open-air cathedral. In the days afterwards, the flowers withered in the jars and the communion rosettes became crumpled. The girls' white gloves took on a patina of dirt.

Doubtless, much of what I liked about it had to do with pageantry. Yet somewhere in the centre of it, there was a sense that life had another element. It went beyond the petty lists of rules and the threat of punishment that was such a strong feature of the catechism we learned off by heart in school. It was a wordless centre. It was a sense of the spiritual, that sense one can sometimes even trace in the lineaments of a person's face or in the look of an eye. It was like a sentence that held in its syllables a truth that was seldom spoken but had become confused with too many other words, too many other sounds.

It was the same with Easter. Christmas is the feast which attracts the greatest popular mythology, but the religious force of Easter has always been greater for me. It is still the feast by which I am most deeply moved. For an over-sensitive boy with a sense of ceremony, it was a time of high drama. I loved it as a religious event, just as I loved the May procession around the grounds of Mount Sion school when a statue of the Virgin Mary, with flowers at its feet, was carried along old paths where rhododendron grew and whitethorn lay in a white crochet on the hedges.

The drama of Easter was the greatest I encountered. Each day in Easter Week had its own tragic script and I entered into it with fervour and anticipation. I relished every detail of the story, from the agony of Christ in Gethsemane to the tragedy of his betrayal and death. The Last Supper was as real to me as a meal in my own house and the cloth with which Veronica had wiped the face of Christ was as tactile to my mind as a tea-towel from our kitchen. If the Corpus Christi procession, like Christmas, had an ornate feel to it, then Easter had the very opposite. If Christmas was a teeming bush of gifts and celebration, then Easter was a bare tree in a cold landscape. It was bleak and empty, like the deserted tomb.

Each day, I entered the Sacred Heart church and dipped my fingers in the font of holy water at the entrance. The stone font was cold against my fingers and the water dribbled slightly down my forehead when I blessed myself. I stood and looked around the church. A purple drape was placed over every statue. The flowers had all been removed.

On Good Friday, the altar itself was stripped down. The church became a bare core of pews, altar and covered statues. In the streets outside, shops closed for the hours of the crucifixion from midday until three o'clock. Earlier, cardboard boxes full of hot-cross buns had been set on the counters. It was a day on which no meat could be eaten. It seemed always grey as if, in my imagination, the very weather was part of the day's drama, conspiring with the purple drapes and the bare church to create an ultimate image of bleakness.

After the Stations of the Cross at three o'clock in the afternoon, the church was filled with people queuing for the ceremony of kissing the cross. The priest stood at the altar-rail and held a wooden crucifix in his hands. After each person had kissed the cold, silver Christ, the priest, with a starched white cloth, wiped the spot which the lips had touched. Then we sat in the bare church and prayed, the silence broken only by the click of a catch as the door of a confessional was opened or closed. Around me, the statues stood behind their purple sheets, blotted out by the magnitude of Calvary.

The spell was broken on Easter Saturday night. Again it was dramatic. At midnight, to symbolise darkness and death, the lights of the church were switched off. The tall Easter candle, into which five grains of incense had been pressed and which had mysterious Greek letters on its side, was lit and the lights were switched on again in a potent image of resurrection. For me, it was a powerful ceremony which carried its fair share of alarm. The church had a primal air when I knelt in darkness. I could smell my father's heavy overcoat beside me. It was the smell of safety.

The Easter ceremonies had a force that contained a truth and that went deeper than rules and the fear of damnation. I cannot say for sure what that truth was for a child. It may have been no more than a bleak, bare statement of mortality and, also, of hope. It was a kind of poetry that affected me deeply. Years later, when I read a statement of Flannery O'Connor's that 'the Church is custodian of the sense of life as a mystery', I thought of those Easter ceremonies and understood what she meant.

Outside of such times, my sense of religion was dominated by terror. At Easter and Corpus Christi, some great statement seemed implicit in the ceremonies. Otherwise, life was a constant battle between the fact of small sins and the threat of large punishment. Looking back, I seemed twisted inside as I wriggled with my morbid conscience. I lived in a world where religion was central. The annual visit by the priest to the houses of the estate meant that rooms were scrubbed and new cups were set on the table where the priest might sit to tea. At night I prayed to saints: Thérèse of Lisieux (the Little Flower, to whose memory my mother had been devoted); Joseph of Cupertino (who helped with exams); John Bosco (who kept me safe). I imagined they appeared to me in dreams. Once, I had a spectacular dream of Heaven. It was as crowded and dramatic as a medieval painting, full of angels and celestial armies. When something was lost — a pen from a schoolbag, a pound note missing from the kitchen window — I prayed to Saint Anthony to find it, and when I found it I usually forgot to say a prayer of thanks. That, in turn, led to a new bout of guilt, and there was nothing for it but to pray to Saint Jude himself, for I was truly a hopeless, damned case.

I would love to be able to say that I grew out of all this but, in truth, I didn't, or I didn't entirely. Childhood is a rib-cage around which the shape of life is formed. As an adult, I read Dostoyevski and found a sentence which said that Hell is the knowledge that one is no longer able to love. That statement made more sense than the terrible, fiery threat with which I had been presented as a boy.

Then, the church and God stood like fathers who eventually would punish their wayward children. Whether this was the case or because I was too hurt and twisted to notice it, I later thought that it lacked love.

At healthier times, I saw religion as a quiet presence. When I accidentally walked into a room where my grandmother was sitting with her beads, praying in a low whisper, I felt as if I was intruding on a private peace. Her brown rosary beads were a fixture of my childhood, together with her lace mantilla for Mass and the cross cut into the crust of her soda bread. Measured against her, I felt complicated, uneasy and uncertain. Each month, she opened the scarlet cover of *The Sacred Heart Messenger*. (I heard of how young women in an earlier decade had rouged their cheeks by pressing those covers to their faces before going to a dance.) Many years later, when I was in my twenties, my grandmother died. I stood outside a white church on a hill above the sea near Dunmore East. As her coffin was carried along a path, I had an extraordinarily clear sense of her lifting from the earth like a bird in flight.

After the age of sixteen, I lost all sense of Catholicism as a positive thing. To the disappointment and hurt of my family, I stopped going to Mass and instead walked around the streets of Waterford or strolled along quays where I stopped near chained railings and watched the Suir. Anger and confusion were all I could sense. I had a feeling of extricating myself not only from an idea but from a community and a supportive structure. I had entered a zone dominated by taboo. Intellectually, I was cutting myself off, though I could not have argued the case with any great force.

I was driven by a sense of wanting to escape some suffocating pressure. On one level, it was a pressure that manifested itself in the constant arguments over social, sexual and moral issues that dominate religious debate in Ireland. I had become aware of such arguments and took whichever side would prove to be most unpopular in my own home. There was also an inner feeling that the world into which I was growing was separated from the trappings

15

of my childhood. I did not leave one certainty for another, but instead entered a void full of questions and doubts. I found that my questions about life were no longer met by the priest's sermons or by the weekly and yearly rituals. Some years before, when I switched on the television and saw students rioting at Berkeley and the Sorbonne, I sensed a movement of revolt and change. It was as if the ripples of a pool had widened to include me. I wanted to challenge the old order in my own way. It was in books that I found a correlative for the way I felt: in Camus, especially, and in his book *The Outsider* most of all. When my grandmother saw me reading *Lady Chatterley's Lover* by D.H. Lawrence and *The Dark* by John McGahern, she said that books were to blame for it all. She was probably right.

To move, then, from that initial childhood sense of ceremony and certainty to a falling away from faith, was to start on a precarious journey. When I was a child, wrote Saint Paul, I spoke like a child, I understood like a child, I thought like a child; but when I became a man, I put away childish things. Some of those childish things stayed with me and I felt caught in the contradiction between them and the person I had become. I experienced the church as an instrument of power rather than as a source of the sacred. A part of me yearned for some relationship with it, but I could not find a meeting-point.

In time, in a monastery in the Knockmealdown Mountains of County Waterford, I found that my story was not unusual. From talking to some of the monks, I learned that they, too, had known just such doubts. For them, the process was part of becoming integral, of uniting the child within you with the adult you had become.

In Mount Melleray, I found again that sense of mystery and presence and depth. I realised as well that, on the positive side, Catholicism had left me with a legacy of seeing people and things as more than just themselves but as potent signs, and that it had imbued the everyday with a sense of the sacramental. This way of looking runs through my world. For the Welsh poet David Jones, this

16

made the Mass the greatest sign of all, and this was a sense that I would come to share.

Yet when I was a teenager, this awareness of a deeper presence in life had become confused with too much that was merely social and negative. Even still, there are many days when it seems lost again. Now, however, it is no longer wrapped in rules. Without it, there is no reason for anything and nothing is in its proper place.

2

It was a long time before I arrived at that realisation. In the years between, I was an apostate and, like any adolescent with literary pretensions, I could read of Stephen Dedalus and take him as an example. It would have been so simple to have rejected a particular religion and then live a life of contentment in another or in none, but it was not to happen like that. My mind was agitated with questions and there was also, of course, Catholic guilt. If you are told in childhood that failure to comply with the rules of the Church will lead to punishment for eternity, then in adulthood the shadow of that threat will linger. The historian Owen Dudley Edwards, writing of Edmund Burke, spoke about Catholicism as a formative influence in ways that I understood: 'The most likely deposit this might have had on his mind would be fear of damnation, associated with schism or apostasy. In cool, calm reflection this would be set aside: later in moments of darkness, doubt, depression, disorder, it could rise high in the imagination.' I knew all about that fevered imagination.

My reason, undeveloped and crude as it was, seemed at war with my emotions. The refusal to attend Mass became part of a pattern that I had adopted and this was, perhaps, common enough in Ireland in the early 1970s as the changes which were taking place in the country were reflected in the lives of its citizens. Unable to make the old and the new fit, I was like a hinge attached loosely to each. Unlike most Catholics of my parents' generation, and in common with many others, I questioned the idea of religion and did not simply accept it as a solid, given force. There were other forces that came under scrutiny at the same time: nationalism was another. I saw my refusal to

18

practise as a form of revolt. It was like becoming a hippy. Yet while I rejected religion, I was still left with a longing for answers to religious questions. In reality, what I rejected was the particularly authoritarian and rigid form which religion had assumed in Ireland. This hid the mystical and relational core to which I would later become attracted. There seemed more anger than reason in my rejection and, if challenged, I would not have found it easy to articulate a non-Catholic position. Likewise, since I was locked within childish explanations, I would have felt foolish and gauche defending the Catholic stance.

This rejection left me with a disturbing feeling of being no longer rooted. My arguments against Catholicism had nothing to do with theology, of which I was ignorant, and everything to do with Ireland. After decades of sexual and political obscurantism, Ireland had started to change in the 1960s. The censorship of books became a thing of the past but, since I wanted to become a writer, it was inevitable that I took on some of the attitudes of those who had lived through decades of censorship. It felt rebellious at the time, but I realise now that many others felt the same. My revolt, then, was conventional in itself.

I found it impossible to take Catholicism seriously and to accept it totally. Those priests and teachers who were its most forceful representatives seemed allied with the forces of authority against which I wished to rebel. I had a particular image of Irish Catholicism as narrow, intolerant and regressive. Such adjectives were like skittles set in rows as I waited to knock them down. I would break out from all this, I told myself. I would have nothing to do with it, I proclaimed. My mind would be open and free.

Yet, with equal fervour, I found it impossible to let Catholicism go. I could trace an analogy in my inability to draw and paint. As a child, I could draw people and houses in simple rectangular or diamond shapes. My talent as an artist never went beyond that simple stage and, to this day, when I draw shapes I produce what looks like a child's drawing. In the same way, my ideas on religion remained locked within a child's framework, lacking any trace of adult intellect. This was not the childlike attitude which Christ praised and demanded. Rather, it was an adult locked into childishness, which is a different and regressive matter. In Ireland, I discovered later, this is not an uncommon situation. For my generation, the first to avail of free education, the problem was particularly acute. A general childishness and authoritarianism kept both the mystical and intellectual aspects of Catholicism at bay. I had a sense of the supernatural, for sure, but it was often clouded with darkness. My reading pushed me beyond the forms in which religion was presented.

I desperately wanted to believe in something. Without a religious belief or confident atheism, I felt adrift and afraid. To those who are never bothered by such problems or who are content with their own belief, this probably seems bizarre and absurd. Yet, for me, it was vitally real. Catholicism had explained the purpose and meaning of life. If I rejected Catholicism, I was left with a need to find another purpose and meaning. At the core, I felt that this question was the most important and that other considerations were secondary to it. I also felt that not many people asked it and I envied what I perceived to be their certainty. Even what might appear to be a superstitious piety seemed preferable to an indifference to the question of what gave life its meaning, and to the question of religious belief.

There was also the paradoxical fact that I felt closer to those who had some spiritual sense than to those who had none or who were indifferent to the issue. I possessed (or was possessed by) a strong sense of the spiritual and over the next few years found myself strongly drawn to different expressions of spirituality. Looking around shops or streets, I saw people going about their daily business and sensed the absolute aloneness of each one. In the face of that aloneness, the question of purpose always surfaced.

One afternoon, when I was an eighteen-year-old student at University College, Cork, I stood in a shop in Shandon Street on the northside of Cork city, and this sense of other people's uniqueness struck me with a particular strength.

I entered the shop to buy groceries. I stood at the counter, casually looking at the shopkeeper as he served other people. There was nothing special about the afternoon, the place, the people, or about my own state of mind. Yet as I watched the shopkeeper, I had a sensation of seeing through him. I saw him as isolated from everyone around him but, with an intensity that frightened me, I also saw him with disturbing depth. He was no longer a mundane part of the afternoon. Instead, in his brown shop-coat and with his head bent as he totted up figures on the back of a white paper bag, he seemed to glow.

In a world wary of transcendence and religious meaning, the language used to express such experiences has either been trivialised or deadened. This was the only time I experienced such an event and I am slow to make any claims for it. In some way that I could not fully fathom, I felt that what had occurred was a religious experience. It was part of the pull between my rejection of the church as a kind of social authority and my certainty of the need for a religious element in my life.

I found that while religious practice no longer appealed to me, the same was not true of religious ideas. Whether in Marxism, Humanism or Buddhism, I had an interest in systems of thought that gave structure and sense to life. I brimmed with questions: in a world without God, how do we judge what is good and bad, and how must we decide to act? If I were to reject Catholicism, was I to leave nothing in its place except an aimless wandering from day to day, buoyed by distractions that took my mind off meaninglessness? If I was to accept it, was I then saying that all others were wrong and doomed? Some of my friends who shared the same disquiet solved the problem by joining the Jesus People or other similar groups who combined a strict reading of the Bible with a hippy vocabulary. I found it an unattractive alternative, every bit as irritating in its certainty as the faith I had discarded.

Half-heartedly and with vague curiosity, I dipped into other faiths. I attended a service in a dreary Baptist hall in Waterford, but lost interest when the preacher said that Padre Pio, the Italian stigmatist, might well be an agent of the Devil. This seemed the replacement of doubt by absurdity.

The way in which such exploration was tied in with rebellion became particularly clear when, in what appeared to be one of the most anti-authoritarian acts of my adolescence, I entered a Protestant church in Dunmore East. The village was the home of my family on my father's side. In summer it teemed with visitors. In winter, it was a quiet place when the hotel closed and rain beat against pub windows.

My grandmother had told me that when she was a girl she lived in fear of what she called 'the gentry'. In one sense, this meant the Anglo-Irish families who lived in some of the large houses in the village or in the countryside around it. More crudely, it meant Protestants. When walking through the village in her girlhood, she sometimes had to step aside to let a member of the gentry pass. In certain instances, refusal to move aside would have meant a blow from a walking-stick or cane. My grand-uncle told me that there were men in the village from whose caps the peak had worn away as a result of being touched when the gentry passed. This all seemed to have happened a long time ago. Nonetheless, it was part of the atmosphere with which, for me, the Protestant church was imbued.

That church, as is sometimes the case in Ireland, stands in the centre of the village, while the Catholic church is situated on a hill at Killea, a mile or so outside. My grandparents are buried in the grounds of the Catholic church and when I walk among the headstones I am startled to see so many names that are familiar to me. These were simply names that I heard around me in my childhood. They are the names of Catholic farmers and fishermen, shopkeepers and women who once waved to me from doorways as I walked to coves.

The names of those who lie in the Protestant churchyard were almost entirely the names of strangers. They carried the vocables of another culture, while the names on the Catholic headstones were more comfortably my own. As a child, the only two things I knew about the Protestant church were its name and the fact that a friend of my grandfather's worked there. It was called Saint Andrew's. The man who worked there was Tommy Ivory, a low-sized fellow who cut the grass with a long scythe. Every now and then he would stop and lean on the handle as he lit a cigarette and regarded the world from beneath the curve of an old cap.

At some point, I was told that it was a sin to enter a Protestant church. This made the exterior of Saint Andrew's seem darker still. The church had a forbidden, if lyric, Englishness about it.

I thought of those who attended that church as people with names like Hilda, Cecil and Algernon, while those who attended 'our' church on the hill had plainer names like Michael, Mary and Ann. By the time I reached my teens, the Protestant church was simply the sum of these facts. When I passed it on the bus from Waterford, I would look through the window and see Tommy Ivory working behind the old wall. I had no desire to enter it — there was no point, after all, in pushing myself to the front of the queue at the gates of Hell.

And yet the day came when I went past Tommy Ivory and past the neat headstones. There was a singer in the village with the alliterative name of Willie Watt and in the early 1970s it was announced that he was to sing at a special harvest recital in Saint Andrew's. I had heard old records of his singing and I had liked it, and I was anxious to hear him in person.

I was no longer a child but neither was I a man, and the desire to see the inside of the Protestant church, and to hear the singing of Willie Watt, became as significant for my intellectual development as the appearance of hairs on my chin became for my physical growth. Accordingly, I entered the church and made my way to a pew. I felt self-conscious in the dark blazer of my Catholic school. I also felt a blend of unease and excitement. My grandmother's strictures on sin were becoming less meaningful by the second.

Like someone who has entered the house of a neighbour who has previously been scrutinised only from behind the twitching corner of a curtain, I had a good look around immediately. I noticed the minister and his strange rig-out, to use one of my grandmother's words. I noticed the cushions and the soft kneelers. I noticed the way men and women bowed their heads deeply in prayer. Try as I might, I could not find a single horn growing from any of the heads, and every foot seemed sensibly shod, with not a cloven hoof in sight. There was a damp smell that was not so much a smell in itself but was the absence of other smells, like wax and incense.

The walls were free of statues but they were not free of memorials. These were a revelation. They commemorated the dead of certain wars that up to then had meant very little to me. Marble and limestone carried the names of local men, many of whom were members of the 'gentry', who had fought in the British army and had been in the Boer War or on French battlefields far from that seaside village. Up to then, I had known of these conflicts from my weekly reading of imported comics such as the *Hotspur* and *Victor*. Now, like the surnames and the accent of the minister, they assumed a visceral immediacy that complicated everything.

Irish nationalism ran deep in my family. My grandfather had fought with the IRA in the early 1920s and, like most Irish schoolchildren in the 1960s, I was familiar with the predictable course of Irish history. The world of Gallipoli and the Somme meant little, while the worlds of Aughrim and Clontarf meant a great deal more. As I stood in that small church, I felt that I was in the presence of something that was more than a religious difference. It was social, political, colonial. It was two pairs of eyes that looked in opposite directions and never met. I was too young to put all this into words. I found myself inhabiting the other side of a question, whereas before I had lived with a cosy answer.

Now, I often think of that first visit when I come on a broken Protestant church in a street or on some country road. Sometimes, such churches are transformed into offices or halls. Some seem to collapse in the countryside, beams sagging from ceilings and rooks flying around panes emptied of coloured glass. A few still thrive with busy congregations. Some continue to exist as churches from which a small congregation leaks on Sunday mornings.

Taking this aspect of religion into account, I think of how sectarian I was in a country where sectarianism kills and of how, with the easy collusion of community, I made ogres of those whose ancestors had fought with my own but with whom I had no need to quarrel. The way in which I saw Protestants was also a reflection of the way in which the very laws of my country saw them. On the day I entered Saint Andrew's church, a gap in me opened and a great deal of light was let in. In religious terms, I was confused. In social terms, that light removed a threat and offered an illumination.

Marxism held many answers that appealed to me and during my university years it became an ideology to which I held. Like Catholicism, it had a language of its own. Words such as *imperialism* and *proletariat* trotted from my lips as easily as the words *penance* and *resurrection* had once done. When I looked at the world around me, I saw much that could be explained in hard Marxist terms. It was the world within that Marxism failed to touch. In that world, I sensed a turmoil and uncertainty that no economic theory could touch or relieve. As a result, what seemed my anger with the world was in essence an anger with myself and my loss of an inner composure. It was if the planet itself was a mirror of inner chaos.

Marxism was faulty for another reason: it dealt with individuals as a social mass. If Marx could claim that religion was the opium of the people, then Marxism had itself become a drug with no shortage of addicts. At its best, it was a theory of society. It explained poverty and exploitation and a great many other things, and it clearly showed the economic nature of so many public wounds. It also illustrated the nature of a dialectic that ran to the core of contemporary society. It explained the problems that were in the world but had no answers for the problems that were in me; and it was these that I was left with at the end. When I woke in the middle of the night and found it hard to get back to sleep, I frequently underwent agonies of conscience about my beliefs. In a space that no economic or political theory could breach, questions lay waiting in darkness.

In the simplistic Marxist terms in which I thought, to attest to such doubts might lead to charges of bourgeois individualism, one of the phrases that I myself threw around like muck from a shovel. Yet once again I could trace this to my rejected Catholicism which put the onus for my salvation firmly on my individual acts. I could not reconcile a spiritual search with Marxist beliefs. Many years later, I heard about priests and theologians like Ernesto Cardenal (who is also a poet) and Leonardo Boff, who could combine both in a theology of liberation, but in my late teens this was not something I could do.

Above all, I would learn about Simone Weil, in whose life social action and religious thought combined to a fine degree. In such people, an inner life and the exterior world come together. In me, there was a split between the two. I envied the clarity of Weil's thought which could confidently express, say, an intense and beautiful meditation on the words of the *Our Father* and, at the same time, maintain a distance from the Church. I loved her writing, with its sense of patience and silence expressed in thoughts such as this: 'When genuine friends of God — such as was Eckhart to my way of thinking — repeat words they have heard in secret amidst the silence of the union of love, and these words are in disagreement with the teaching of the Church, it is simply that the language of the market place is not that of the nuptial chamber.'

Yet while the words and example of Simone Weil and others could attract and hold me for days, I would soon feel my mind wander again and I would enter that mental region of confusion, anger and uncertainty which made it impossible for me to attend church ceremonies. I was coming to realise that the world of religion was not going to leave me alone. To the extent that I understood it, I identified with the mystical side of Simone Weil. When calm, I felt that, like her, I was 'waiting for God'.

More often, I felt like Sisyphus pushing a heavy stone up a hill again and again, only to have the stone roll away before I reached the top. In a book by Albert Camus that captivated me in 1975, the myth of Sisyphus became a title and a theme. It began: 'There is but one truly serious philosophical problem and that is suicide.' Camus said that what he described was an intellectual malady. It was an unhappy time in my life and this may have had something to do with my enthusiasm for such books. For others, God was in his heaven and all was, if not quite well with the world, at least in its proper place. I had a sense of things shifting and of uncertainty. I read in Rilke that we must love our questions, and that statement seemed a solitary consolation set like a stem in a vase. If I was certain of nothing else, I was certain that I had a great many questions.

While I knew of many others who felt the same way, it did not seem like a widespread condition. Years earlier, the Second Vatican Council, which began in 1962, had unleashed a maelstrom. At its most immediate, I saw this change when Mass was said in English instead of Latin. Nuns now wore different habits or no habits at all. Priests played guitars and often tried hard to be hip. Older people like my grandmother looked on in dismay and incomprehension.

The Vatican Council had been called by Pope John XXIII. I was only six at the time but the effect he had upon me has always illustrated to me the effect that adult events can have upon children. I can truly say that I loved him. Round and fat, with eyes that his secretary described as autumn-brown, he looked out from newspapers and magazines and the very photographs transmitted

27

something which appealed to me. It was a kind of simplicity. Somehow, his papacy was an exercise in love. He was part of a great change about which I knew nothing, but his presence was so potent that I was affected deeply. After he died in June 1963, I imagined his ghost lying on a bed in my house like the figure in the last photograph taken of him. He seemed at once ordinary and special, and the sense of his impact has never left me. In the world of my childhood, he seemed a bright star of hope. I saw his photograph on many kitchen walls, often in a mottled cardboard triptych which included the assassinated brothers, Robert and John F. Kennedy.

By the time I ceased to practise Catholicism, I was far from the spirit of Good Pope John, as many people in Ireland called him. He was part of a change that was taking place in many facets of life. In Ireland, in myself, this led to a clash between two worlds: between, say, my father's memories of a priest pouncing on lovers in ditches after a country dance and my own sense that life demanded a fuller, more generous-minded and less vindictive explanation.

I missed church ceremonies, but felt it hypocritical to attend them. Catholicism, like most religions, offers a structure that takes in not merely birth and death but permeates the pores of everything that lies in between. As surely as the seasons, it provided a pattern for the time of year: the spring renewal of Easter; the Marian flowering of May; the sombre, dark remembrance of the dead in November. Year after year, my own life followed these patterns. Now that I had stopped practising, these patterns were gone too and there were times when I felt as if I had moved to another planet. This was sometimes a frightening feeling. Where once there had been a place and a reason for everything right down to the smallest act, there was now a void.

It was not enough for me to have stopped practising. I felt that to have stopped and left it at that would been simply another form of smugness: the smugness of certainty replaced by the smugness of indifference. It would have been intellectually dishonest. Yet as I moved from one small church to another, or as I pondered Camus' words, I felt only a sense of deepening doubt. In retrospect, the single unfortunate part of my rebellion was the terrible bitterness with which it was tinged at certain times.

Against this questioning, I was developing as a writer. I wrote mainly poems, some of which touched on religious themes. In the early 1980s, I was invited to give a poetry reading at Newtown School in Waterford. This school, as far as I knew when growing up, was a Protestant school. I had never been inside its gates, though I had passed it often and looked with interest at its high walls and trees which hid the school from view in a posh part of the city. There were rumours that the girls who attended the school were sexually precocious. When I saw pupils from Newtown walking around the city, the main thing I noticed was that their accent was different. It was what I regarded as a Protestant accent. I had heard that some well-known people, like Conor Cruise O'Brien, Erskine Childers (the former President of Ireland), and the writer Dervla Murphy, had sent their children there.

Newtown had a reputation as a liberal school and I was looking forward to reading my poems there. The reading went well and, after it, I heard from a teacher that the school was not a Protestant institution. It had been founded by the Society of Friends, or Quakers as they are more commonly known. I knew nothing of Quakerism but was intrigued by what I heard. At meetings in the school, for example, no votes were taken. Instead, a consensus was reached. Quakers, I was told, regarded such votes as likely to lead to conflict. I picked up other shards of information: that Quakers were pacifist; that they refused to bargain and that their price was arrived at fairly. Above all, I learned that, for Quakers, silence was of the utmost importance.

This element of Quakerism had a particular appeal. My most intense experiences had a quality of silence and solitude. This may have had its roots in a childhood where, for much of the time, I felt solitary and apart. Later, I would find this quality expressed in the lives of monks. I would find it as well in people I admired — for example, in Dervla Murphy, whom I once interviewed for a newspaper at her home in Lismore, County Waterford, and who lived a self-contained life that had about it the external rigour and interior richness of a medieval anchorite's.

Attracted by the idea of silence, I began to attend Quaker meetings in Cork. There, the Society of Friends met at Summerhill South every Sunday morning. It was unlike any other religious service or meeting that I had attended. In a bare room, a small crowd gathered and sat in silence. The silence had a quality that changed as the hour drew on. It had a personality and a character of its own. It started out as a gradual settling, a quiet broken by the sound of coughs and adjusted coats. Long pews surrounded a table on which some flowers were set in a bowl. There were no statues or glittering ornaments; no priest or altar or confessional. There was just the room and those who sat in it.

After the initial period of restless adjustment, the silence of the meeting took on a deeper character. As it grew, I realised how, despite my deep need for it, I spent little of my life in silence. While I could argue intellectually about the social role of religion in Ireland, it seemed that the very core of religious belief did not lie in such arguments but in what happened when I sat in silence at such meetings. It was an experience I knew elsewhere: in coves and on cliff-tops, for example, or in a corner of a field near a country bridge outside Saint John's Park where I once disappeared into Wordsworth's *Prelude*. In some way, it was also connected to my experience in the grocer's shop in Shandon Street.

This brief experience of silence on Sunday mornings became very important to me. It was an oasis of quiet to which I looked forward. It had its own language and expression. As it intensified, some of those at the meeting would stand to speak 'as the spirit moved them'. When everyone was settled into silence, it was said that the meeting was 'gathered'. Not all those at the meeting were

Quakers. Visitors like myself were known as 'attenders' and these included a small number of people who practised other religions — at least one family, for example, attended the meeting on their way home from Mass. The theology of the whole business had little interest for me; it was enough to share the silence. I wrote a poem about this experience:

> *Silence takes over the room.*
> *As if gathered for a sign, they dispatch*
> *Business and let the moments pass.*
> *On tables, in bowls, flowers bud*
> *Like phrases about to be said.*
>
> *Outside, their acre of graves*
> *Shows names and dates like the flat*
> *Covers of shut files. Terraces close*
> *Around them, dogs restless in yards,*
> *Children at windows catapulting birds.*

I liked the plainness of Quakerism, its stress on inner motive and outward action, its refusal of blame and its loving acceptance of others. Moreover, it somehow seemed to accommodate uncertainty. The historical record of the Quakers was impeccable: in ambulance corps or as organisers of creches in Northern Ireland prisons, as suppliers of food during the Famine or of comfort to prisoners, they had filled a middle, necessary role.

Their ability to avoid conflict was startling. I received an illustration of this after I was asked to write an article for a Quaker magazine. In the article, I criticised the look of many Quaker meeting-houses. I thought them ugly. I presumed that the article might lead to some argument and contention. Instead, a number of Quakers shook my hand and thanked me for my opinion. Needle-like in my views, and sometimes bristling with restlessness, it was not quite the way I was used to doing business.

31

I loved to walk in the small cemetery behind the meeting-house. It was unlike any other graveyard I knew. There were no ornate tombs or displays of sculpted marble. Instead, there were rows of plain headstones. It seemed as simple and moving as military cemeteries near the sites of battlefields.

I learned that, as with the Sunday meeting, there was no fixed service for Quaker funerals or weddings. They had the same format: people gathered in a room and spoke from the silence.

Among the plain headstones, I felt how the quality of life and quiet lived once by those who were buried there lasted beyond their death and gave a character to the place. It was the same experience I would later get from ruined monasteries, as if the grass and stones contained the lives that had been lived there and were themselves a shape which prayer had taken.

I wondered about becoming a Quaker, but joining up had little attraction for me, and at any rate I felt too aggressively full of contradictions. Likewise, the emotional pull of Catholicism was still strong in a negative way and I could not envisage becoming something else. Where Catholicism appeared a closed system, Quakerism seemed open and kinder. It was enough for me to experience the weekly silence, and to find an expression of spirituality that satisfied a deep need in a way that was not oppressive.

In time, I no longer attended the meeting, but I never forgot the experience, and the memory of those shared silences is still potent. It did not translate into certainty: instead, I found a site where my uncertainty was stilled for a little while and where, with the flowers on the plain table, I felt at home and at ease.

3

In 1985, after spending two years on the dole, I became a freelance journalist. Up to 1983, I had worked as a part-time library assistant in Cork and, for a time, as a spectacularly unsuccessful part-time teacher. Restless and unsettled, I found that journalism gave me a chance to approach people and situations in a way that brought them into focus. The articles I wrote reflected my interests: interviews with writers and artists; book reviews; radio talks on everyday experiences. Life was looking up: I had the chance to meet people who interested me and, frequently, the questions I asked them were a reflection of my own inquiry. My work as a journalist was a passport into other people's experiences. I could measure them against my own.

My method of working was simple. Journalism was a way of making money but I also used each article as a way of buying time in which to write poems. Each week, I sent a list of proposals for articles to various editors in Dublin. If the ideas were of interest, the editors usually made contact within days. I had a good relationship with most editors and found that living in Cork was a distinct advantage. There, I was free from legendary tantrums and from office politics.

I worked well with one editor in particular: Deirdre McQuillan, a supplement editor with the *Sunday Tribune*. She commissioned me to write a number of lengthy features. In one of my letters, I proposed writing an article on the lives of the monks who lived in Mount Melleray, a Cistercian monastery in the Knockmealdown mountains in County Waterford. She was immediately enthusiastic.

I was very excited at the prospect of my visit. My enthusiasm was fuelled by my general interest in spirituality and also by my love for the work of Thomas Merton, the American monk and poet. I had became aware of Merton in 1982. During that year, one of the most despairing I had known, I spent a long period in hospital and found that many of the books which normally pleased me were suddenly of no interest at all. Only two writers fired me: the novelist Francis Stuart, and Thomas Merton. In Merton, I sensed a person who had asked some of the same questions as myself and who had found answers in a life spent in silence on the margin of American society. Like the monks in Mount Melleray, he was a Cistercian. Among the many things I loved about him was the way he combined ordinariness with silence, and wrote of religion with sharp and studied insights. I disliked the triumphalism of his early books (and especially disliked his auto-biography, *The Seven Storey Mountain*), but I excused this work as the highly charged zeal of a convert. Nonetheless, there was something in the tone of his work that, in the words of a Quaker phrase, spoke to my condition.

On a Friday in July 1984, I began the journey to west Waterford. The first I saw of the monastery was a grey church set among dense trees against a backdrop of mountains. I had been looking out for it since leaving the town of Cappoquin. A signpost outside the town, set at a point where the road divided, pointed to the monastery. The town itself was quiet, its main street showing few signs of life on a summer evening. Some men stood here and there at corners; a woman pushed a buggy along the pavement and stopped to look in the dark windows of closed shops.

Once, there had been a busy bacon factory which gave work to many in the town, but it had closed. The character of the town changed. I had never thought of it as affluent but it at least had an air of business and, when the factory went, this appeared to lessen. There was less money about and, for the young, there was less reason to stay.

Cappoquin lies a few miles from Lismore, another small town. Lismore is dominated by a castle, owned by the Duke of Devonshire. The castle is a grey pile overlooking the Blackwater and it gives the town a feudal impact. Approached from Cappoquin, the castle and the river seem like an image from a lost England, a country Camelot rented out by the famous. Those who have stayed there include the film star and dancer Fred Astaire. The poet John Betjeman visited the castle as well and, while there, wrote a love-poem set in the town of Dungarvan. Its refrain refers to Dungarvan in the rain, and those small towns can be bleak places on a rainy day. On winter evenings, the windows of small chip-shops steam up and, at weekends, the most popular pubs are busy late at night.

Lismore has shops which seem lost in time, the fascias and fronts lingering like props from a film set in Ireland during the 1950s. There are remnants of the Anglo-Irish outlook in the countryside between Lismore and Cappoquin. Walls mark the borders of demesnes. Wide gates, some of them rusted and fixed firmly in gravel, stand at the entrances to long avenues.

The countryside of west Waterford has many relics of the Anglo-Irish world. They became a kind of folklore surrounding my visits to Mount Melleray. The landscape and the countryside had its own story to tell, and the story of the monastery blended with that tale. Rusted gates stand open at the entrance to demesnes. At Villierstown, a village lies behind gates. Near Portlaw, a town built by Quakers and constructed originally in the shape of a hand to honour the idea of toil, visitors gather bluebells in June near Curraghmore, the home of the Beresfords. The Beresford family was once said to exist under a curse. A series of seven tragic deaths occurred over many generations after a demented old woman made a curse in revenge for the death of her son who had been flogged to death at Curraghmore in penal times:

'You and yours accursed will be,
You can't escape by land or sea,
For death will strike you suddenly —
Beresford, oh Beresford!'

The landscape has more benign aspects. West Waterford is a countryside of local loyalties. These loyalties revolve around politics or sports, or around success stories like the athlete John Treacy, who grew up in the village of Villiers-town and became a world-champion cross-country runner. The names of county hurling teams are bandied about in homes and pubs: Lismore, Brickey Rangers, Ballyduff-Portlaw whose most famous player was Tom Cheasty. I saw him play when I was a child, his burly body filled with power when he took a sideline free or barged through opposing players before facing the goalmouth and driving the ball into the net with the force of a bullet. Unlike soccer players, who leap and embrace each other after a goal, Cheasty just walked away and continued playing as if scoring the goal was simply part of the job.

Such people and places were part of my mental image of west Waterford. I now placed the monastery among them, like a new piece of furniture in an old room. While I acted as if this was my first visit to Mount Melleray (or plain Melleray as most people called it), I had been there in my childhood. Then, I travelled the roads of west Waterford on a bus tour. The bus on which I travelled was the height of new technology. I was delighted by the circular nozzles under the luggage rack above every seat. When I turned the nozzle in a certain way, a small, firm gust of air was sent into my face. I stood on the seat, closed my eyes and turned my head towards the circle of wind. There were small lights as well, worked by cylindrical plastic buttons that clicked when I pressed them.

The bus slowed near some wide gates that stood across the road from a shop and near some small houses that lined a wide avenue. Yet this was no Anglo-Irish entrance. Deep in the mountains, this was the entrance to the monastery.

The bus entered the gate and began to ascend the steep avenue, past a grey school on one side and fields of crops on the other.

At that time, I had no understanding of monasteries. When the bus stopped near a large car-park overlooked by statues of saints, I got out with everyone else. I remember little else about that visit. I was taken to the monastery shop, where I got my first sight of monks: quiet-spoken men in black-and-white robes. The shop was filled with pictures and objects that many might see as tawdry, but which for me, as a child, were filled with pious potency: images of the Sacred Heart similar to the picture over the fireplace in our kitchen; the Infant of Prague; the tilted head of a grieving madonna.

I was given a gift which a monk held in one hand as he made a blessing with the other. It was a rosary ring, a silver ring with a small cross and a number of notches around its edge. I was told that such rings had been worn by people in another century when it was illegal to own rosary beads. Instead, a rosary ring was slipped on one finger and, as the prayers which made up each decade of the rosary were whispered, another finger moved from notch to notch until each had been touched and ten *Hail Marys* recited. At that point, the small cross was reached and it was time to start turning the notches full circle again for the next round.

I have one other memory of that day. With other people from the bus, I was guided across a wide patch of tarmacadam and then along a stair which had a smell of church about it. I arrived at a balcony which looked down on an altar and on rows of dark wooden choir-stalls. I was ordered to keep quiet, and an adult's thick fingers pressed against my lips to indicate silence. The monks, it seemed, never spoke. Not only that, but they kept to themselves and, with the exception of a few like those we had seen in the shop, they had little contact with the outside world. It seemed an awesome idea. It was said that they even dug a little patch of their own graves every day.

It was to this monastery that I was now returning. I had little luggage. I had written to the abbot a few days before and had told him the purpose of my visit. He replied by return, welcoming me to the monastery. A photographer would arrive separately. The article, with its three pages of text and pictures, lies beside me now as I write. One of the photographs shows monks working in a kitchen. Another shows a monk standing near a wide pond that has the contemplative atmosphere of a Zen garden. The monk near the pond is Father Kevin Fogarty. In time, we became friends.

In some ways, my enthusiasm exemplified the contradiction of my religious stance. I felt Catholicism to be a stultifying force from which I wanted to escape and yet I was drawn in some strange way to this most Catholic of places in the mountains. I was like a fish trying to wriggle out of a net and I mistook the wriggling for real escape.

The same was true of my attendance at the Quakers' weekly meetings. There were other instances as well. At Saint Gobnait's graveyard near Ballyvourney in west Cork, where a cracked cup lay on a stone near a holy well, I made the rounds of an ancient pilgrimage. The centuries of pilgrimage had given the place an atmosphere to which something in me responded. Miles away, in the hills around Gougane Barra, I climbed and thought of monks who had lived there many centuries ago. In the small oratory on the island, I watched candles flicker as the wind whistled through the barely open door.

In certain moods, I added to a small store of books on the spiritual life. Like the places to which I travelled, they were of a certain kind. Together with books by Merton, there were others on sects and groups which treated silence as a central aspect of life and in whose organisation there was often a blend of the spiritual and the artistic, though they would not have called it that: the Amish people of Ohio, Pennsylvania and Indiana; the Shakers, whose simple furniture became fashionable among the rich in London and New York in the late 1980s. I relished the way the Shakers knew that a spiritual belief was reflected even in dancing and cooking, and that the most ordinary gestures are reflections of an inner life.

Other books dealt with Zen Buddhism, a subject to which I had been led by a Merton essay. Some told of people in whom I detected the same impulse despite my uncertainty and unbelief. Eric Gill was among them, a sculptor, typographer and stone-carver who founded the artist's guild of Saint Dominic and whose life combined a sometimes frenzied and controversial sensuality with the discipline of the monastic life and the work of an artist. My picture of Gill had been formed in the years before Fiona McCarthy's biography revealed him as a complicated figure who had had a sexual relationship with his daughters. Those revelations did not change my enthusiasm and admiration for those parts of Gill's life and philosophy that mirrored my questions.

Ludwig Wittgenstein was another such figure, a philosopher whose spare, trimmed sentences seemed rooted in the silence in which he often lived. It came as no surprise when I learned that he had once thought of becoming a monk.

Thoreau was yet another, and his life near Walden Pond became a landscape that I could easily inhabit in my imagination. It was the same with Simone Weil. There was also the medieval anchoress, Julian of Norwich, a woman whose extraordinary, simple writing combined clarity with belief and love. Her words, unlike the work of many inferior writers, seemed as immediate as a sweeping-brush or the hard shell of a nut.

Such figures became strands of a single impulse. When I went back to Mount Melleray, they all came together. They were part of the mentality I took with me and the monastery became a correlative for my interest in them, a precise metaphor for all that attracted me to their worlds. In the attitude and life of the monks, in their sense of solitude, silence, prayer, study and work, I found the most complete expression of what this instinct meant. I did not feel any sense of conversion, but instead felt an illumination that here was the proper space for my questions, my need for silence and, perhaps, for a kind of spiritual peace. Like the Celtic monks whose poems and miracles I loved, I had a sense of life as pilgrimage, poetry and presence. Increasingly, I ceased to think of pilgrimage as being a journey to a particular place and instead thought of it as all of life, and that particular places were special sites along the way, set there like lights on a map that I had seen in a Cork museum, that lit up when buttons are pressed.

The car stopped near the monastery church. I got out and then, having sought directions from one of the people strolling in the grounds, I entered a small door set in a wall near a garden. Passing a quiet fountain where gold-fish swam, I saw immediately that it was a place which, given my nature, I could easily romanticise, just as one could romanticise the idea of monasticism itself and imbue it with a saintly hue. This romanticism was often detrimental: it has played havoc with the memory of Thomas Merton, for one thing. Merton hated the idea of being canonised by popular enthusiasm; he believed that those who turned him into a saint would have been better off looking into themselves. I was anxious not to make the same mistake with Mount Melleray. To do so would be to create a false picture of the place. It would also be a source of trouble for myself, for little in my everyday life could match an idealistic image of a self-sustaining community. Were I to construct such an image, I would not be adding depth to my own search, but would be setting up the monastery as an escape hatch from the humdrum, often unhappy world. I would have to be on guard.

Close to the path where the fountain stood, the guestmaster met me and guided me to the tiled hall of the guesthouse. He shook my hand. A friendly, warm man, Father Joseph Walsh spoke in low tones, but there was nothing about him that indicated a contempt for the real world.

'Isn't Seán Kelly after doing great in the race?' he said. Kelly, a champion cyclist from the town of Carrick-on-Suir in County Tipperary, had become Ireland's latest sports star. We talked about him for a few minutes. The monastery bell boomed. It was six o'clock and time for vespers. Father Joseph gave me the key to my room — number 19 — and left for the church, his hands folded within the large white sleeves of his habit. 'I'll see you after tea' he said. 'There's a few biscuits on a plate in the kitchen if you're hungry until then.'

I climbed a wide stairs and found my room. I unpacked and, weary and delighted, listened to the water in the fountain outside the guesthouse. It had been easy enough to get here. I thought of those Greek monasteries which one can enter only after a monk agrees to haul the visitor up in a net connected to a pulley. My own arrival had been more mundane, but the reasons behind it were complicated. I was here to write an article but, more than that, I was here as part of the spiritual search that dominated so much of my thinking and for which I lacked so many of the words. Now that I was here, I kicked off my shoes, lay back on the bed, and felt as if I had entered silence itself.

4

The following morning, I awoke at eight and, shortly afterwards, went for a walk in the hills behind the monastery. I followed a thin path and eventually came to a summit marked by a cross. I could see the countryside around me. It was easy to mark the difference between the fields cultivated by the monks and the rough acres which were still untamed. A crude landscape had faced the first monks who had settled here.

After breakfast, I went into one of the old school buildings near the avenue that leads to the monastery. There, I saw a slide show that told the story of how the first monks had arrived. Slides clicked and shifted in a projector at the back of a large bare room where visitors wandered. Many stayed for a few minutes, watched part of the slide-show, and then left. Others saw the show through.

In a hallway outside the room, some old, official-looking sheets of paper were pinned to the wall. These were lists of rules for a Leaving Certificate examination held in the years before the school, run by the monks, had closed down. Some of the words were in Irish, written in a Gaelic script which I had once learned in an infant class before it was discarded for a standard, less interesting type. I had seen the same script on old manuscripts: an ornate whirl of curlicues, dots and slanted accents. Like the words *scriptorium* and *vellum*, it was one of the images I associated with early Irish monasticism.

As I read the old examination rules, I heard the voice-over in the room behind me. It was sometimes accompanied by music: a deep, polyphonic chant that is immediately associated with monasticism. I loved that sound.

I learned the story of Melleray's foundation from other sources which included a booklet I found in the monastery shop. The shop sold statues, prayer-books, pictures and other examples of religious objects. Most of them were tawdry. Yet once, in west Kerry, I was in a house which had belonged to a Blasket Islander. The walls of one room still held old, smoke-stained pictures of the Sacred Heart, together with an image of Mary. In that rough, dark setting, the pictures had become one with the spirit of the place, set there like icons that had absorbed and strengthened the spirit of those who had lived there over generations.

An old monk worked behind the shop counter as I moved among the objects. Plastic pens, showing different monastic scenes, were stacked in a rack on the counter. I looked at cheap key-rings which displayed a picture of Mary, Queen of Heaven. Eventually, with the booklet in my hand, I approached the counter. The old monk worked as I waited, a piece of leather over one finger as he twisted and shaped a strip of wire with a pliers and made rosaries with dark beads drawn over the wire.

This was Brother Gerard Leddy, the oldest monk in the monastery and, when he died aged 99 in 1992, the oldest Cistercian monk in the world. He told me he came from Araglen in north Cork, and that Eamon de Valera had stayed at his mother's cottage in 1917. Years later, he met de Valera, who often came to Melleray to visit. Dev, he said, had remembered the taste of his mother's beautiful scones.

I found him easy to talk to. The old monk did not admit to any nostalgia caused by the mention of such homeliness. He told me that he had joined the monastery in 1914. On his way to Melleray, the children of a local school crowded to a classroom window to wave goodbye to the young man off to join the monks. Earlier, he had stood with his father as a girl took a photograph. At the entrance to Melleray, his mother had wept. It took him some time to adjust to the spirit of the monastery and to the strict routine, which demanded that the monks rise at two each morning and keep silent for most of the day. Brother Gerard found himself perplexed by many of the changes which came into monasteries after Vatican II but, in time, he adjusted. Each day, he told me, he worked in the shop or in the garden, never neglecting to undertake physical work — an essential part of the Cistercian life.

He mentioned to me that a monk called Ailbhe Luddy had written a fuller history of the monastery. Others spoke of this man and at least one monk thought of him as the originator of a Melleray myth. This story had its genesis in the visit by H.V. Morton, the English travel writer, who went to Melleray in the 1930s. Morton was not very taken with the experience; instead, he seems to have been uncomfortable and uneasy during his stay. I suspect he may have been more serious than the monks thought was good for him. He saw a monk digging and, when he asked what the monk was doing, was told that the man was digging his own grave and that this was something every monk had to do each day. Morton believed the story and cited it in an account of his travels around Ireland. I have often heard it repeated. The story had only a fragment of truth, since it was a Trappist custom to dig a small section of ground after a burial. This served as a *memento mori*.

A similar myth is discussed in James Joyce's story 'The Dead'. One of the characters, Mrs. Malins, talks of how her son is about to visit Mount Melleray. Reference is made to the hospitality of the monks and to the bracing air around the monastery where 'the monks never spoke, got up at two in the morning and slept in their coffins'.

In a manner that set more emphasis on the truth, Ailbhe Luddy recorded in his book that Mount Melleray had been founded by Trappists in 1832. Driven by an impulse that I did not fully understand, I absorbed his story just as I absorbed the atmosphere of the place in which it was based. This was more than just the usual research involved in writing an article. It was a kind of reclamation, as if by knowing the story of Melleray I would take in its past as well, and this would help to focus its attraction for me within my struggle with Catholicism. I read of how the Cistercians had been founded by Robert of Molesme in France in 1098. They had broken away from the Benedictines whose rule, devised by Saint Benedict, the new monks wished to follow in stricter detail. A further transformation occurred in the seventeenth century. It was brought about by Cardinal Richelieu's godson, the sybaritic Abbé Armand-Jean de Rancé. As a young man, he fell in love with the Duchess de Montbazon. She became ill. According to legend, he went to Paris to visit her but she died before he arrived. Entering her room, he was horrified to find that she had been decapitated. Her coffin was too small and, to make her fit, an undertaker had chopped off her head. That sight changed de Rancé's life: he fled to a monastery called LaTrappe and, in 1664, instituted a monastic regime of fierce austerity. The Cistercians who followed him became known as Trappists, or Cistercians of the Strict Observance, and this is the order to which the monks in Mount Melleray belong.

An Anglo-Irish landowner in County Waterford, Sir Richard Keane, offered to rent a stretch of mountain land to the monks who had originally arrived in Melleray from France in 1831. He gave them 600 acres. It was mostly crude, untamed territory. Its Irish name, anglicised as Scrahan, meant rough land. There was hardly a tree in sight; harsh winds blew without interruption over the mountains. I read of how the land could be cultivated but would demand an immense amount of hard work. Its isolation made it attractive in ways that I understood, since, for certain temperaments, the desire for solitude is an essential aspect of a religious life. A farmer might look at that land and find few positive things to say about it. It was ideal for the monks. A small group settled originally in a small game-keeper's lodge that still stands near the monastery. They called it Bethlehem, as if within it lay the birth of a miraculous idea.

The setting-up of the monastery gradually became a kind of communal activity. Villagers came together and walked over the mountains to help with the work: 400 men marched from Modeligo, 800 came from the town of Cappoquin, 200 came from Lismore. Crowds walked from Ballynoe in County Cork and from Knockanore and Newcastle in Tipperary. They dug and defined the outline of the monks' farm, often starting work with them at dawn, and working through the day.

The next step was the reclamation of the land. Rocks were hauled out and the soil was prepared. Thousands of trees were planted. Walking around the place now, it is hard to imagine it without trees. It was only when I walked away from the monastery, over towards the spectacular area known as the Vee or towards the village of Newcastle, that I saw what those first monks had to face — a bare, mountainy landscape broken by flashes of heather or grey outcrops of rock with nothing between earth and sky. On winter afternoons, that sky over the Knockmealdowns appears sometimes to have a watery bleakness, as if to match the mood of the mountains. At such times, the landscape becomes the epitome of desolation. It drives one inward.

That sense of unity between monks and landscape exists everywhere in the monastery grounds. In this way, I learned that the place is not simply a set of buildings where monks live, pray and work. The monastic sense permeates the fields, the paths and the people who walk them. Over the few days of my visit, this sense of unity in the place contributed towards the creation of a sense of unity in myself. The story of the place became part of the story that I was writing but also of the other, interior story that I was trying to understand. I have always been affected by landscape but here I was affected in a particularly intense way. I understood what the old Celtic monks meant when they spoke of two landscapes, one physical with its rocks and mountains; the other sacral and intensely connected with spirituality.

The monks gradually altered the face of the mountain-side and changed the character of the area. This did not simply concern the farmwork or the fresh acres that delineated what had once been scrub and rock. It is a mood, an ambience, a quality of silence and prayer that marks it out from other places. It is a quality that visitors notice.

Afterwards, I learned that I could recreate it in my memory with an overheard fragment of monastic chant or by the words of a psalm. Ordinary as the monks can seem in their conversation with visitors, there is still an extraordinary atmosphere about their lives and monastery. I found myself drawn into it. At its deepest, it was far from my old arguments. It transcended my conflict with the institutional church. It was rooted in prayer and silence rather than in rules and strictures. Oddly, I had little trouble with the idea of prayer and a great deal of trouble with the intellectual idea of God. I still felt that in quiet prayer some resonant communication took place. As time went on, it moved beyond words and ended in the heart of silence.

With the stones they had dug up, the monks continued to build. They built a church. A refectory was added. A guesthouse was constructed as well and, here, the monks maintained the monastic tradition of not turning away anyone who came to the door. Daniel O'Connell was among those who stayed in the guesthouse and his visit in 1838 was remembered for a long time. His stay was a powerful symbol, for Mount Melleray was the first monastery established in Ireland after the passage of the Catholic Emancipation Act, (of which O'Connell had been the main architect), by the House of Commons in 1829. Filled with religious ardour and, perhaps, with guilt after a duel, O'Connell swore to come back every year for the rest of his life. He never came again. I met others who were more persistent and many guests told me of their need to visit the monastery once a year, to simply switch off and stay there for a few days.

In 1924, the writer Evelyn Waugh also paid a visit. He criticised the objects in the shop, but praised the manner in which services were held. In his diary, he wrote that it compared well with a Mass he had attended in Glenmalure where the priest had belched into the chalice.

Much of what I learned about the monastery emerged later as images or themes in poems. One story which affected me in this way was set in 1839. Then, the potato crop had failed and heavy demands were made upon the monks' charity. The following year, the blight continued and famine spread. Father Kevin showed me a long wooden box set against the wall in an outhouse. In the 1830s, it had been used to store meal which was then given to the many starving people who called to the monastery. At first, only a few people came, but the numbers grew as the famine became worse. Many came from those very villages which had helped with the founding of the farm. Vincent Ryan, the abbot, ordered that no one was to be turned away. He was leaving for England to visit the monastery of Mount St Bernard but, before he went, he made sure that the wooden bin was filled with meal. According to the legend, he stopped in Dublin on the way back and preached in a church, making a plea for money to help his community where, he felt, the food would have nearly run out and where indigence was always a prospect.

He arrived back in Mount Melleray and found that the food in the bin had not diminished in the least, though hundreds had been fed from it. The bin, a symbol of abundance, was kept and, for a long time afterwards, people were given meal which had been stored there.

I read that the monks opened a school in 1843 and of how, nearly ninety years later, a convent of Cistercian nuns was founded at Glencairn, a few miles away. In 1935, work started on a new monastery church, its walls made from stone that had once been part of the walls of Mitchelstown Castle, an Anglo-Irish fortress in a town through which I had often passed.

Monks try to be self-supporting and this was achieved by running a farm. Balanced between work, prayer and reflection, the monk's day, to a casual visitor like myself, often seems centred on the farm and the church. A monk told me that, long before the philosophy of opting out and living on the land became popular, the early monks realised that a link exists between the countryside and an inner life. If they produced too much, they could give it away to those who had too little.

If the monks working in the fields are far from the church when the bell is rung for the Office, they will pause and pray where they stand, turning off the tractor or putting a chainsaw to one side. I saw a monk working in a field when the bell rang for the 10 am Office of *Terce*. He stopped work and prayed where he stood, his head bowed, his hands resting on the handle of a spade while the bell boomed across the acres that separated him from the church.

The monastery continued to grow and it attracted many novices. In the years since my visit in 1984, there have been roughly 75 monks living there. Father Kevin told me that there were 120 when he joined. Standing together in the choir, they seem mostly old men, many of them in their late sixties. There are a few novices, but the numbers have fallen.

Walking along the avenue near the old school, I found it hard to imagine Mount Melleray with few or no monks. It would seem a strange progression from the time when those first monks came, as if the monastery had been suppressed by a force more subtle than any King Henry VIII could muster. Walking among the ruins of old monasteries, I have thought that even the broken stones retained something of the atmosphere that had once informed the lives there. The broken stones of Mount Melleray would contain a certain sadness as well.

5

I was to stay in room number 19 many times. At first, this was simply coincidence but, after a number of visits, I specifically requested this room. I liked it for its view of the guesthouse garden and the distant fields, and for the susurration of the fountain outside. There were other sounds: a dull gunshot to scare birds from crops; the heavy shifting of gravel as monks or guests walked on the path below my window; the bark of Mel, the abbey dog.

It was a simple room and I like simple spaces in which things have an order of their own. The furniture was basic: a bed with loud springs in its mattress; a wash-basin with a towel and a small tablet of white soap; a writing desk and two chairs. A crucifix was nailed to the wall. A lamp stood on the table and a reading-lamp was affixed to the wall over my bed. A wicker wastepaper basket stood on the floor near the table.

At first, the room had a slight air of dustiness. The bed was freshly made and I learned that the making of one's bed afresh is a task given to visitors at the end of their stay. The guestmaster supplies blankets and sheets, and one guest makes the bed for the next.

Some coat-hangers were hooked in rows on a rail. When the window was open, they jangled in a mild breeze. Like much of the monastery, the window had a Gothic look to it, curving and coming to a point at the top like the tip of a cowl. Seated at the desk in the mornings, I could hear footsteps on the gravel or a tractor in the fields. And, always, I heard water pouring with a steady rhythm into the fountain. When working hard, I lost my sense of that sound, but when I stopped and stretched my fingers, I suddenly heard it again, a background sibilance that helped me to settle.

The sound of flowing water sometimes possesses a calming power. Unlike the noise of a car, say, it is one of those sounds that inhabits silence without destroying it. Teresa of Avila felt that convents should be built near water. This was not just for purposes of sanitation; it had as much to do with her belief that the presence of water is an aid to contemplation. When Thoreau lived at Walden Pond, he reflected that when one is out for a walk, one often strays, without even knowing it, in the direction of water. I heard the monks sing of water when they chanted Psalm 22:

> *Near restful waters he leads me*
> *To revive my drooping spirit.'*

On a hill behind the monastery, a small stream, due to some quirk of gravity, gives the illusion of running upwards. It is a frequent topic of discussion among guests, one of those themes that help to break the quiet in a dining-room filled with people who are strangers to each other.

The monks never turn anyone away and Father Joseph was the ideal guestmaster, caring for those who stayed but never intrusive. One evening, I talked with him about how some people might draw an unfavourable comparison between monks and people outside the monastery, between a life of action and a life of what seems a passive silence. This is the contrast between Martha, who busied herself when Christ called to her house, and her sister Mary, who sat at his feet to listen. Joseph quoted Angelus Silesius: 'The rose transmits its scent without a movement. I have a definite feeling that if you want us to experience the aroma of Christianity, you must copy the rose. It irresistibly draws people to itself and the scent remains with them. A rose does not preach. It simply spreads its fragrance.'

This contrast between contemplation and action was something of which I was clearly aware. Part of the problem that religion presented me with took the shape of an unease between my everyday life and my interest in spiritual matters. I felt split rather than whole. The story of Martha and Mary increased in resonance as I reflected upon it and, at times, felt more like one than the other. In particular, I was fascinated by Mary's silence. In 1994, I wrote a poem called *Sisters*:

Martha

Her mind a packed picnic basket,
A woman so busy she calls
Boys by brothers' names and longs
For hours alone in olive groves.
Her dreamy sister hunkers near the low —
Voiced visitor whose talk she'd follow
If goats were gathered and basil plucked.

Mary

To sit in silence and listen
As pots chortle and oil in urns
Warms near a sunlit doorway —
An act more simple than frisking
Crumbs from aprons, or arching
A fine finger in trails of dust:
And yet like this to enter history.

On my initial visit, I was fascinated by the small details of monastic life, such as the fact that there is no fixed charge for guests. A polished table, with some envelopes stacked on it, stood near a mirror inside the hall door of the guesthouse. Guests place what money they can afford into one of these and then slip the envelope into a slot outside the guestmaster's room. There are no names on the envelopes. The monks never know how much has been paid by a particular guest or even if anything has been paid at all. There are no invoices and no receipts. This is one of many monastic features that challenge the ethic one encounters outside. The spirit of the monastery and its Rule are composed of such details.Whether in its challenge to the idea of constant chatter or in its assertion of the necessity of prayer, the monastery — all monasteries — represents a kind of sublime affirmation of the spiritual. I sensed that, like poetry and birdsong, spirituality is essential but has no basis in economics or in the idea of material use or profit. In this way, the monastery questions many contemporary attitudes and outlooks. The spirit of monasticism is utterly unlike most of what seems to drive the everyday world. Like certain writers, the monks live at an angle to that world, but are not contemptuous of it.

The guests eat together in a dining-room, three times a day. The food is prepared by monks, but they do not sit with the guests. It is simple food: porridge and cereal for breakfast; meat, potatoes and another vegetable, followed by dessert, for lunch; in the evening, a light tea of beans and toast or a small salad. The atmosphere is usually relaxed and the monastery itself is one of the great themes of conversation over meals.

All kinds of people come as guests. At lunch on my second day, I met an English Buddhist who was travelling from monastery to monastery around Ireland and Britain. His journey was a kind of pilgrimage, a *peregrinatio* which had no ultimate destination. He told me of how he had visited the Carthusians at Parkminster in Sussex, an order which, for Thomas Merton, preserves the authentic monastic tradition. Each Carthusian lives in a hermitage within a shared charterhouse. One of the rooms in each hermitage is known as the Ave Maria, a small space where monks stop to pray before leaving or entering their cells.

I first heard of the Carthusians when Liam Miller, who published my first book of poems at the Dolmen Press in 1985, sent me a copy of Guigo the Carthusian's letter on the solitary life. It was translated by Thomas Merton. Guigo lived at the Grande Chartreuse in the twelfth century. The solitude of which he wrote still has not changed within the Carthusian spirit and many of his sentences should please anyone who is fond of solitude and silence. Not surprisingly, the Carthusians are not members of a large order. They are strict about those admitted as monks. Guigo's letter is a kind of song to solitude and I took to it immediately. In Merton's translation, it has lines like this: 'I esteem him happy above all who does not strive to be lifted up with great honours in a palace, but who elects, humble, to live like a poor countryman in a hermitage, who with thoughtful application loves to meditate in peace, who seeks to sit by himself in silence. For to shine with honours, to be lifted up with dignities, is to my judgement a way of little peace, subject to perils, burdened with cares, treacherous to many, and to none secure.'

While not every guest has an interest in such matters, I think that most people who visit monasteries come with a desire for silence. Thomas Merton felt that nowadays people turn their backs on silence and that a life without silence cannot be full. The silence of monks is legendary, though it is not as dominant a feature as I had expected. The monks in Mount Melleray are no longer silent all the time and the Great Silence now lasts only from eight thirty at night to eight in the morning, a period during some of which the monks are at any rate asleep. The presence of silence, of course, continued a line which I had started to draw at Quaker meetings. It was the opposite of the sociological clamour.

With the exception of prayer-time, the silence in Melleray was once total. One of the monks showed me some examples of the sign language which was developed to communicate in those silent centuries when monks spoke only during the Divine Office or at Mass. To splay the fingers downwards like a fan was to make the sign for water. He told me that he preferred the old sign language 'because talking is such a slow way of telling things'. Another monk, Father Columban, told me of how two monks from Mount Melleray were once in hospital in Cork. They were in adjacent beds and, when they conversed, it was the first time they had spoken to each other in sixteen years.

While I learned that the rules on silence have been relaxed, the monastery is still a quiet place and silence is as much a part of its personality as the buildings or the chanted Office. Few of the monks speak loudly and most of those I met are economical with words. Words, like anything else, can be wasted if there are too many of them; and, as I knew myself, too much talk can be a form of evasion. Eloquence can hide more than it reveals. In such instances, silence is an unwanted form of confrontation.

The first word of the Rule of Saint Benedict is *Ausculta* — listen. Certain monks gain a reputation as good listeners and problem-solvers. I have even been told of monks who are mind-readers, though I think this has more to do with empathy than with magic. One who spends a great deal of time in silence, and who has crossed his or her own personal desert, would be able to tell much about another person very quickly.

Most of those I met stayed for two or three days and many had simply come for the weekend. Some stayed longer. My visit as a journalist lasted for three days but since then I have stayed for as long as a week and have gone at least once every year. Guests are asked to do very little or nothing at all, though many help out when they can. Some lend a hand in the kitchen after meals. There, one of the jobs I enjoyed was shaping butter into spheres. Boniface, who looked after the cooking, gave me two wooden spats with striations on one side and showed me how to roll a lump of butter between them until the butter became solid and round. By doing such work, I became less engrossed with myself and entered the simple, mundane round of the monastery.

The guesthouse stands just behind the church. To get there, one enters a wooden door set into a wall. This wall marks the boundary of the enclosure or that part of the monastery into which the public cannot enter. Much of it is out of bounds to guests as well. Father Kevin took me on a tour when I was writing my feature article. He guided me down long corridors and around the small farmyard, through workshops and the refectory, into the library and the monk's own rooms. The rooms, like those in the guesthouse, are simple: a bed, table and chair, books, a cupboard. Crucifixes, or pictures of Mary or the saints, were nailed to workshop walls.

Since monks take a vow of poverty, they own very little. For many years, it was the custom that a monk should be buried without a coffin. A cowl was folded over his face and the corpse was placed in the grave. The absence of a coffin symbolised poverty, but it was upsetting for relatives, who were not always comfortable with such a sight. Kevin showed me old photographs of such a funeral. What struck me most was the face of the dead monk. It had not been tampered with in any way, as is the habit in funeral homes now, and it looked very different to faces to which chemicals and cosmetics have been applied. It looked truly a *memento mori*, a real death's head.

Kevin told me that his own decision to become a monk came only after years of ordinary living. Like others to whom I spoke, he was answering an inner call: 'God wanted me here.' Kevin's room is packed with books. Like myself, he gets every excited about books and praises Rilke, Patrick Kavanagh, or a book on Zen and art. He always speaks in low tones and I find it easy to listen to him. Likewise, as with most of the monks I know, I can be silent with him. Like those old Irish monks, he is very fond of the natural world. Those Celtic monks, he said, blended asceticism with a love of nature. One without the other would have made them too soft or too hard.

Often, I reflect on how I love silence but, after my first hours visiting the monastery, I found silence difficult. Silence has its own dangers and monastic silence becomes an enveloping mood. Silence also has its own pace and I soon realised how rushed my days can be. I walked quickly around the monastery grounds, though I was going nowhere in particular; it was as if I was moving from one experience to the next with nothing in between and without reflection on what I was doing. The silence became a serious issue at around ten o'clock on the evening of my second day. The wooden gate at the entrance to the enclosure had been locked and the monks had been in bed since 8.30. Some of the guests were drinking tea and chatting around the fireplace in the guesthouse for an hour or so. Others went to bed early since there is little to do. The guesthouse had no television or radio. There seemed little to do except go to bed, yet I felt eager for distraction. I began to wonder what exactly I was doing in such a place. I was unable to sleep and lay awake listening to the fountain, bemused at myself for the absurdity of my attraction towards silence and my inability to practise it. I wanted to be distracted from the questions that rose in me like a troublesome yeast. I felt drawn towards all that the monks represented, and my clichés of opposition were crumbling. At its mildest, this was uncomfortable since the aggressive mental framework of years was falling apart.

I presumed that other guests can have the same problem with silence. I found a similar experience recounted in Patrick Leigh Fermor's book about monasteries, *A Time to Keep Silence*, published in 1957. He writes of a visit to a French abbey where the first four days of his stay were gloomy periods of lassitude. His sentences find an exact echo in my own experience: 'The desire for talk, movement and nervous expression that I had transported from Paris found, in this silent place, no response or foil, evoked no single echo; after miserably gesticulating for a while in a vacuum, it languished and finally died for any lack of stimulus or nourishment.'

Leigh Fermor describes a great tiredness that came upon him and I too experienced this: an urban exhaustion as parts of myself unwound and I became immersed in the mood and meaning of the monastery. He wrote that when he left the monastery and returned to Paris, he had the opposite problem. I have experienced this too. It was as if I carried the memory of the monastery in my mind and the everyday world of family, children and work moved at another pace, full of situations that got in the way of the calm I took from Mount Melleray. This was probably the result of an unhealthy romanticism but, whatever the cause, it created problems for a few days.

Within certain limits, the monastery guests can observe their own hours but, once, I tried to keep the same hours as the monks. They now rise at 4.45. On my first night as a guest, the bell boomed across the mountains and woke me. I looked out the window and saw a darkness so complete it lacked a single star. The quiet was immense. The bell was ringing for Vigils, the first Office of the day. Father Kevin explained that the monks gather in the church for this Office and it is a vigil kept in the night. I did not go to the church but, after throwing water on my face, sat at my desk and wrote. It was a joy to work at such an early hour. From what I could hear, it seemed that no one else was awake in the guesthouse and my mind felt free and empty, a necessary state if I am to write well. On such a morning in the monastery, I wrote a poem which I never had to revise. It came clear and true, floating on its own melting as Robert Frost said a poem should. This has not happened very often.

The bell boomed again at 7.15 and it was time for the monks to attend Lauds. I stopped working. It was cold. I put on my coat and went for a walk in the fields. At 7.45, for the first time in years, I went to Mass. To get to the church, I passed through the guesthouse kitchen and then along a corridor within the enclosure. Monks stood in meditation here and there in the cold corridor. They wore white robes and seemed as still as chess-pieces. When the time for Mass drew near, they entered the church and I could hear the swishing of their robes.

It was even colder in the church. During the ceremony, the monks stood around the altar and guests were welcome to join them there. I found this hard to do since I had resisted all forms of religious ceremonies for years. After a few minutes, I decided to stand at the altar as well and soon I settled into the ceremony. It was an atmosphere imbued with a sense of the sacramental. I found that, at last, I could differentiate between sacrament and structure. 'What frightens me', wrote Simone Weil, 'is the church as a social structure.' Like many Irish agnostics, I had spurned the social structure. Now, in the presence of the Eucharist, I felt in touch with a core of sacredness. Tension gave way to ease.

After the ceremony, I went back to my room and tried to work again but could not, and it seemed as if some murk had cleared. I went for a long walk. The air was crisp and sharp, as if the cold blade of a knife was pressed against my face. In a field beyond the guesthouse garden, a hare, startled by my steps, bounded in front of me and sprang away. I stopped. The hare stopped again. I coughed. The hare bounded away again. I stopped. The hare stopped too, tense for another sound. I moved my foot. The hare sprang over beds of cabbages into the trees.

I reached to the branch of a tree and shook it. Dew dripped loudly from its branches when I plucked a chestnut. It was large and green like some underwater craft from a fantasy. I split the soft shell and examined the polished nut that fitted perfectly in a cross-section of the shell. Near a ditch, I saw a robin perched on a stone. In the distance, I saw clouds on the mountains. I felt at one with everything. I could see why so many Irish monks wrote small nature poems in the margins of manuscripts. By the time I got back to the guesthouse, it was time for breakfast.

The monk's day follows a set pattern of prayer, work, study and silence. It seems a very balanced life and does not reflect those divisions that are reinforced elsewhere. Most monks, for example, study and also do some physical work. Again, I discerned a balance which I lacked in myself. It was not an imbalance that upset me but, like the unease between Martha and Mary, it displayed another aspect of the way I was mishandling things.

I read over the Rule of Saint Benedict and felt that much of it could as easily apply to people like myself who lived in a pattern different to any that monasteries contained. I liked the way Saint Benedict refuses to become ethereal or pious and is always immediate, as concerned with the cups and jugs in the monastery kitchen as he is with the meaning of the gospel. He seems an earthed man. The monastery, he said, was 'a household of God'. The Rule is rooted in ordinariness and this, for me, is one of its most attractive aspects. My old image of Catholicism saw it as a structure which had little time for the ordinary and was more concerned with the enactment of strictures. Like the poetry of Patrick Kavanagh (who wrote that 'ordinary things have lovely wings'), Benedictine and Cistercian life places the ordinary and the sacred within the same realm. This was yet another division within myself that I now felt could be healed. Years later, when I learned of the French missionary Charles de Foucauld and read his ideas on the importance of Christ's years in Nazareth, I sensed again that fusion of the everyday and the holy.

In one sense, little seems to happen in the monastery. Yet time passes quickly there. Father Kevin told me that this is something which all monks experience and it is a knowledge within which one's own life can seem quick and small, like the flight of that sparrow through the mead-hall to which Bede compared the span of a life.

In some ways, every day in the monastery is the same and this predictability became a challenge to another of my standard demands: that there must be constant variety and change, and that monotony is undesirable in any form. The Office will always be held at the same hours. The food does not vary much, though the monks are no longer prohibited from eating cheese, milk and eggs. Monks are sometimes given meat to help them recover quickly from illness. The monks' clothes have been the same for centuries, a black and white habit that seems impossibly heavy on hot days.

Compared to the way many people live, all this seems unbearably repetitive and marginal. Yet I felt that its very predictability holds a clue to its power. Such monotony is a room within which the monk lives out an inner idea. Within silence and order, the monk draws closer to God.

When I saw it like this, I realised that monastic life is not an escape from life but a deep confrontation with it. Applying this to myself, I saw that I was refusing to allow such a confrontation to take place in my own life. There is something bare about the life of a monk. All the props and scaffolding have been removed. I gathered that the illusions of novices are quickly stripped away. In this way, monks do not dodge the world but face it at its very centre which lies at the core of each person's life. I have heard it said that monks must have an easy life, free from mortgages and unemployment, with little to bother them. I have also heard it said their life is a useless one, an escapist route for emotional people. While this may be true for some of those who try to be monks or nuns and who apply to join the monastery, it is surely not the case with those who stay. It is a difficult life in which one faces one's own particular demons head-on. And, as Patrick Leigh Fermor wrote, it is only a useless life if one rejects the efficacy of prayer. I now find it impossible to make such a rejection.

Guests are welcome to attend the Office in the monks' church and I went as often as I could. There is a smaller church, which I disliked. Guests enter the main church through a door which leads to rows of pews marked off by a wooden barrier. Behind it, the monks face each other across the aisle. While one can see the monks, one cannot have a clear view of the entire church since one's view is blocked by the back of an organ. In this way, the distance between monks and outsiders is maintained.

The Office is enacted eight times each day. The monks stand in their choir-stalls and wait for the abbot to tap a stick against wood. This is the signal that the Office is to start. Each Office is a mixture of prayer, singing, and chanted psalms. The quality of the chant varies; sometimes, I thought it sounded uneven, as if a collective tiredness had come over the monks after their day's work. At other times there is a rich blend as voices and spirit move in unison. The chant once consisted entirely of Latin words, but now it is mainly in English.

Hearing the monks recite the Office gave me a new awareness of the Psalms. Each day has its own psalms and the numbers of the psalm for a particular day are listed on a sheet of cardboard close to the public pews at the back of the church.

At each Office, the monks also recite other prayers. These include the Gloria, during which they bow. They often bow deeply, bending the upper body and not just lowering the head. Such a bow reminded me of a story in Carl Jung's autobiography. A rabbi was asked why no one now sees the face of God as people once saw it. The rabbi said: 'Because nowadays no one can stoop so low.'

During the Office, the Psalms are sung from side to side of the choir, each couplet sounding through the church:

> *They go out, they go out, full of tears,*
> *Carrying seed for the sowing:*
> *They come back, they come back, full of song,*
> *Carrying their sheaves.*

For Thomas Merton, the Psalms were a tabernacle made of words. There is a psalm for every mood and situation: for love and grief; for loss and praise; for anger and bewilderment. The psalms became very important to me as examples of work that connected poetry and spirituality. Rhythmic and sustained, the images stayed in my mind as ciphers of religious experience and perception:

> *You stretch out the heavens like a tent.*
> *Above the rains you build your dwelling.*

> *You make the clouds your chariot,*
> *You walk on the wings of the wind,*
> *You make the winds your messengers*
> *And flashing fire your servants.*

Their recitation each day weaves the Psalms seamlessly into the monk's life. Like the Office itself, they are part of a monastic rhythm that is itself linked to the days of the week and the seasons, the whole combining in an ancient structure within which the monk lives out his life.

After my first two nights in the monastery, I decided that Compline was my favourite part of the Office. On a later, winter visit, I liked it even more when the church was darkened and a small light shone behind the altar near a high, stained-glass window depicting the Virgin Mary. The monks were again dressed all in white, as for the early morning Eucharist. Compline ends with the chanting of *Salve Regina*, an ancient antiphon to Mary, which is sung in the manner of Gregorian chant. The words are in the original Latin, the language blending beautifully with the close of day in monasteries around the world:

> *Salve, Regina, mater misericordiae,*
> *Vita, dulcedo, et spes nostra, salve.*

I think of Compline as an Office for the Virgin Mary, a figure who was once known in Irish as 'little white-necked one'. The realistic intimacy of such phrases, which I also found in the work of Julian of Norwich, struck an immediate, loving chord. It was an aspect that seemed especially strong in Celtic Christianity. It was also a feature that had been lost in a dense dust of legalisms and shalt-nots. Like the world of Orthodox Christianity, it was something which had been hidden from me. In the *Carmina Gadelica*, a remarkable collection of Gaelic poems and songs from Scotland, I came across expressions of belief that had the realism of everyday life but a sense of the transcendent as well.

In the light of this, I came to feel that religion was something which had been stripped of its sap by the way it was treated in Ireland. I could see an analogy in the case of the Irish language, an extraordinary force that had been revived with enthusiasm and then murdered by narrow-mindedness as it became allied with negative forces. Now, poets and others were rediscovering Irish and freeing it from such forces. I felt that I wanted the same thing to happen, for myself, with Catholicism. With my childhood memories of John XXIII, I sensed that excitement but it had dissipated. Now, in monasticism, within a force that had been strong for centuries, the process began.

Having heard *Salve Regina* in the dim church, and then watched the monks leave silently in single file, I sat in my pew for a few minutes and meditated in the quiet aftermath of the antiphon. By the time I reached this state, I felt at ease with the silence and myself. I had stopped rushing around with my mental baggage and my need for a new experience every five minutes.

By then, it was 8.30 and the day was over for the monks. On the way back to the guesthouse, I walked through the dark garden and saw the headlights of a car on a road in the distance. They seemed like a glow-worm, flickering and then fading away. Night settled on the monastery and on the mountains. At last, I felt quiet in myself. It was a long way from my anger with sermons on Sunday or from my innumerable arguments with Catholicism.

For a moment, I felt as if I knew what the whole thing was about and, deeply, I felt part of it.

6

In the years that followed, I went back to Mount Melleray a number of times. It became a quiet haven to which I frequently retreated. Yet while I loved the world that I found there, and while I recognised that such a world was grounded in a particular set of religious beliefs, I still could not bring myself fully to practise as a Catholic. I went through bouts of attending church ceremonies but never kept it up for very long. Something in me always held back. Like Simone Weil, there was much that I loved about it but still I could not go the whole way. I understood what she meant when she spoke about the point of intersection 'between Christianity and all that was not Christianity'. No matter how regularly I attended church, I never gained a sense of my search having come to an end. I was to find other places that were sources of inspiration. They also became a rich expression of my inner world.

The most moving of these experiences occurred in 1993 during a visit to Paris. The experience was pivotal and my final doubts crumbled before it. At last, I accepted. I still felt the force of the arguments about so many issues, but now I would argue, with love, from within and not, with hatred, from without. I was staying at the Irish College in Paris and was there for a short period in order to write. For reasons that were not entirely clear to me, I had a slight sense of going there for other reasons as well. This sense of following a sub-conscious pattern was not new to me. At times, it can seem uncanny and I try to remain true to it. There is something intuitive about it that I sense is important. In the weeks before, I had been thinking a lot about the monastic and mystical elements of religion towards which I was drawn and the practical element in which I lived and worked. At its crudest, it was a gap between solitude and parenthood; silence and wordy busyness; between the cloud of unknowing and the murk of knowing a little about too many things in my work as a journalist. It was the old opposition between Martha and Mary. When I arrived at the Irish College on the rue des Irlandais, I unpacked my bags and met the acting administrator, a Dominican nun named Marie-Humbert Kennedy. I asked her about the old churches of Paris and she suggested a few which I might like to visit. She mentioned the church of Saint Severin, for example, which I had intended to visit anyway since I had read that Eric Gill had liked its stonework and atmosphere. She also suggested the church of Saint Gervais which lies in the Marais behind the Hotel de Ville, just a few minutes walk from Notre Dame and its cavernous darkness broken by the light of a thousand flash-bulbs. I kept this church in mind as I went about my business, much of which, coincidentally, took place in the Marais, for it is there, among the old Jewish streets and the small stationery shops with hand-made paper displayed in windows, that part of the book on which I was working was set. Each morning and evening, I worked on poems and prose, and I read the only book I had taken with me: T.S. Eliot's *Four Quartets*. I had underlined particular sections. The lines I had emphasised included these, from 'Little Gidding':

> *You are here to kneel*
> *Where prayer has been valid. And prayer is more*
> *Than an order of words, the conscious occupation*
> *Of the praying mind, or the sound of the voice*
> *praying.*

When not at my desk, I walked through the streets or idled in cafés. I had been to Paris a number of times but something had changed for me. When I went first, as an aspirant writer in my early twenties, I entered a myth. It was the myth of artistic Paris, of bookshops like Shakespeare and Company and of cafés like Les Deux Magots. Since my late teens and my first reading of Camus, I had been in love with the idea of Paris. Now, in my late thirties, I found that something had changed. Places which once interested me seemed dry and dead. I had no interest in the myths of others. I felt that I would have to create my own Paris and that it was this which would be most truly reflected in my own writing.

On a Sunday morning in June, then, I set out for Saint Gervais with all these things in my mind. I had heard that the church is used by a monastic order known as Les Fraternités Monastiques de Jerusalem. I had never heard of this order. I was late for the ceremony, yet from the moment I entered the church, I was drawn by the nature of the way in which Mass was celebrated. The monks and nuns, attired in white, sat or knelt in rows before the altar where a number of icons were set and where candles stood in a menorah. Hundreds of men, women and children sat on chairs, leaned agaist wide pillars or simply sat on the floor. The church, one of the oldest in Paris, has a rather tattered air as a result of long closure. This added to the sense of visiting a kind of catacomb.

The Mass was conducted with great care. The ceremony was a mixture of knowledge and love. There were elements which were strange to me: at the *Our Father*, for example, the monks and nuns raised their arms to Heaven. At the point where people make the sign of peace to each other (a moment that is sometimes met in Irish churches with a wriggling embarrassment), the organ was played with exhilaration and the members of the monastic community moved through the congregation with a true joy. The singing — and the Mass was almost entirely sung — was especially beautiful. The whole affair combined elements of the Roman, Judaic and Byzantine traditions but, it remained a ceremony where nothing was trendy or shallow.

Without drama, I can say that this hour and thirty minutes in Saint Gervais was among the most moving and joyful experiences that I had ever known. I felt that the experience, at this particular point in my life, was akin to finding a precise word which was waiting to be named. One of the more exciting moments in making a poem occurs when dozens of words are hurled away and the correct one is suddenly found. My experience at Saint Gervais was like that.

Later, I learned a little about the order. It was founded in 1975 by Pierre-Marie Delfieux. A former chaplain at the Sorbonne, Pierre-Marie had spent some years living as a hermit in the Sahara, continuing the tradition started by those hermits known as the Desert Fathers. He became convinced of the need to found a monastic order in the city. The huge cities of today seemed to him to be the equivalent of the desert. The order now includes almost one hundred members of many nationalities, with more nuns than monks and with many novices. An explanatory leaflet declares that the church of Saint Gervais "has been entrusted by the Cardinal Archbishop of Paris with the task of growing into a contemplative centre." I met some of the monks and nuns, among them an American, Brother Bradford, and an Irish nun who lives as a hermit.

Monks and nuns live in separate buildings close to the church. The monastery is based in the lower two floors of a large apartment block close to the Monument to the Unknown Jew. I had lunch there with Bradford, as everyone called him. We sat in a crowded refectory where monks and guests ate in silence. A monk placed a record of Handel's *Water Music* on a turntable and the flowing melodies accompanied our meal of ratatouille during which not a word was spoken but for *Grace* at the start and finish.

This order is deliberately based in the city, just as much of Christ's life was lived in the city of Jerusalem. I found this enormously relevant and attractive since sometimes monasticism is sentimentally seen as a kind of religious pastoralism that denies the value of urban life. As someone who has always happily lived in cities, I immediately responded to this effort to create a sense of contemplation in an urban world. I discovered that the lives of the order at Saint Gervais are not a simplistic outcry against urban life. Rather, they say that they want to 'recognise all that is truly beautiful in the city, its creativity, its yearnings and its innermost values, singing through these the praise and the glory of God.' At the heart of Paris, I felt that this order had touched what Eliot, in the book I was studying, called the still point of the turning world.

On the way back to the Irish College, I felt a terrific excitement. I had found the focus where Paris and my inner self met. I had discovered once again that, despite all my arguments with the Catholic Church, there are signs of tremendous tenderness, excitement and promise. Some are social; some are liturgical; some are monastic. The best of them begin in an interior space that has been shaped by silence and prayer. On that Sunday morning in Paris, I came into contact with that space as it manifests itself in an urban form.

I went back to Saint Gervais a number of times. Each day, I sat with others before the icons in an oratory and then joined the monks and nuns for vespers and mass. It was an experience that seemed at once marginal and central. In that worn church by the Seine, I learned with Eliot what it was to kneel where prayer has been valid, and I felt again that prayer is not simply a matter of words but is often wordless, gathering an accretion of quiet as it deepens and grows. I learned that I could keep this core of silence in my life just as this order keeps it within the heart of Paris. I realised that I had been making the mistake of seeing contemplation and activity as alternatives and that I was creating an unecessary schism in my mind. Now, I saw them as united, one within the other and running through like it a seam.

That Sunday evening, when I sat at my writing-table and looked across the damp roofs of the Latin Quarter, I knew that I had experienced something that would remain in my memory with the force of an icon in a quiet room.

7

The effort to write down the story of my spiritual search
has proved difficult. I found a problem of language with
regard to religion, just as there is a problem with regard
to the language of politics. In one sense, this should not
have seemed strange since a great part of monastic life and
mysticism (the two elements towards which I am strongly
drawn) is built around silence and not around words. The
very word 'God' draws reactions that vary from the
enthusiastic (a word which itself has an etymology rooted in
the Greek word 'enthousiasmos', meaning 'possessed by a
god') to indifference, embarrassment, cynicism and contempt.
In religion, as in politics, there is a jargon to which my ears
have been closed for many years. I found that I lacked the
words for religious experience, and that the experience was
more real than the language in which it is conventionally
expressed. I felt isolated from the language used by those
who detest religion and also from that used by those who
practise it with evangelistic fervour. I kept in mind the
answer given by the novelist Vladimir Nabokov when an
interviewer asked him about his religious beliefs: 'I know
more than I can express in words, and the little I can
express would not have been expressed had I not known
more.'

Some of my friends and acquaintances had little or no
time for religious ideas. Like my younger self, they associated
it primarily with a negative set of social forces. The
psychological aftermath of the damage caused by such
forces is still a strong feature of life in Ireland and it colours
a great deal of religious discussion. Such discussion, among
people over thirty who are opposed to religious ideas, is often
marked by a kind of tired agenda from the 1960s. It is as

predictable and dated as the agenda to which it is opposed. It sometimes seems to be a type of neurosis caused by the gap that exists between childish involvement and adult resentment. I recognise this gap in myself and it was only after my visit to Melleray that I began to make sense of it.

My visit made many things clear; it had the force of a conversion. I had not become a compliant Catholic; rather, I saw faith practised in a way that was unsullied by the weight of social pressure and argument, and I felt that at the heart of the monastery lay an experience and faith that matched the heart of my own life, and that could be sustained despite the occasional absurdities of the church as a social entity. It was an interior experience and it changed everything. By temperament, I cannot be rule-driven. I still find it hard to take part in religious practice, but from time to time I no longer feel alienated from the core of what the Mass contains. That core is radical and affirmative and deep. It contains both suffering and hope, and it survives despite the attitudes and deadness that frequently surround it. The Catholic Church, at the moment, seems less exciting than the mystery and love which, despite everything, survives at the heart of it. There is a new energy stirring at its edges — among women, among contemplatives, among people for whom the old ways have broken down — and I suspect that before long this energy will become the centre. In Ireland, the Church has slowly become more human.

As with Melleray, my visit to Saint Gervais became a tangible experience for much that was wordless and silent. Later again, I spent some days at a Buddhist-run conference and retreat centre on the Beara Peninsula in west Cork. There, at Dzogchen Beara, meditating before wide windows that looked out on the sea, I entered the heart of silence again. I drew a lot from the Buddhist idea of constant change and impermanence and saw the relevance of such a belief to the changes in my own temperament and search.

A great deal of what such places and experiences represent for me contradicts much that is elsewhere the norm. It breaks the consensus on many issues in ways that

71

are not new but are still striking. On a simple and obvious level, the contemplative life illustrates a point of view which has no regard for money or social status as measures of worth. Likewise, the attitude towards guests is a perfect example of solidarity. In striving for silence, monastic communities confront the constant din that dominates much of life. By building a life around work, prayer and study, they exemplify a balanced life. Karl Marx spoke of the degrading division of work into intellectual and physical labour; such a division is challenged by monasteries. The monks at prayer in the church in Melleray would be recognised by peasants from France or Italy in another century. There is a time-lessness about the sight of a monk working in a field or standing in an arched, cold cloister, with narrow windows through which the sun shines in even lines. Such an image is at once appropriate for a medieval monastery in Ireland or an obscure abbey in a French forest. It is timeless, but time itself is one of the questions that the religious attitude raises. It is said of prisoners that they serve time; in the same way, monks serve timelessness. We all do.

I have met a few people who live in monasteries for long periods. They never become monks, but the world of the monastery is one they instinctively understand. Some of them build their day to match the timetable by which the monks live. Set between darkness and sunset, the monk's day has a different arrangement to the days of those who live outside. It is an arrangement of which I often think as I go about my business at home or in the city. Moving between work and family, between the demands of fatherhood or making a poem, I no longer see a contradiction between the nature of my spiritual search and the actuality of my life. As monks like Bradford can remain at the heart of Paris, spirituality can remain at the centre of what I do — hidden, searching for new definitions, eccentric even, but there nonetheless.

When Cistercians retire at 8.30 each evening, many people are getting ready to go out or to settle down before the television for the night. And when they rise at 4.45 each morning, most others will sleep on for hours to come. In this way, the monks appear to follow a different pulse. The world at that hour of the morning can be at its most lonely for those who lie awake, tossing and turning in the night. It is an hour at which many people die. Yet in the monastery, it is the start of a new day. Vigils, the first Office, sets the day in motion. The hours of the Office, like the monks' clothes, fit a centuries-old pattern.

The monks still do many things then as monks have always done them, and in this way I sometimes think of the monastery as a spindle around which the world turns. By maintaining patterns that are centuries-old, the monks are among the most conservative people one could meet. Yet many of those very patterns go against the grain and so there is also a sense in which monks are radicals. They seem, in some ways, close to a communist ideal or to a commune. They are not in it to make profit and they live in a group where each person's particular talents are used to the full in the service of others. They give away much of what they earn by their work to those who have less. They opt for prayer where others might choose indifference; and where many people either treat religion as a set of moral blinkers, a rulebook, or as a dated artefact to be disdained, monks assert that to live a spiritual life is to reach the core of being human.

With the years, I have found that the silence of the monastery is among its most vital attributes. Paradoxically, this sense of Melleray's silence was sometimes revived by sound — by a record of Gregorian chant, for instance, or by the words of an old Irish poem. I learned that worthwhile silence is not just the absence of noise. It is also the absence of distraction and of a mental busyness which prohibits the creation of an inner quiet. Silence is not a passive or quietist quality but an active one. It is a necessary stillness. Moreover, I found that by going into silence I often created an atmosphere in which poems could be written, as if silence had become words.

I am aware of silence from the moment I enter the monastery. It is tactile, like the pages of a book or the texture of stone. Within it, I walk, sit and reflect. When Thoreau sat by his fire at night near Walden Pond, he grew more aware of the sounds around him — birds calling in the darkness, branches crackling as animals stirred and scurried. I have sensed such things in the monastery and I have learned that such sounds do not distract from silence but actually become part of it. In this way, I have accepted silence as an interior quality that shows itself even in the way a person walks or listens. I have watched monks walking alone in the garden or in a street in Paris, and something about the way they moved indicated that they inhabited a reflective quiet, even when walking quickly.

There are other kinds of silence. Silence can be a sign of neurotic introspection, creating a deliberate barrier between oneself and others. It can be a weapon of non-cooperation. It can be a sign to indicate disapproval or indifference. It can be a measure of discomfort, as when two people shuffle uneasily in each other's company and fish wildly for words. It can be a sign of incomprehension, unwillingness, anger, disbelief. It can be the result of terror or unkindness.

Monastic silence is closer to the silence of lovers. The early Cistercians called monasteries 'schools of love'. In Paul Eluard's poems, reference is made to the gaze of lovers, to eyes that watch each other in silence in a space beyond words. Much of what is felt at such moments is in the realm of the wordless and even of the incomprehensible. I sensed this silence in an old monk who sat in the church with his eyes fixed on the tabernacle above the altar. Plants shielded him from the gaze of the congregation and he simply sat there, his hands folded within the sleeves of his habit as he looked straight ahead.

I found that to live without such an inner silence seems like an amputation of some vital part of myself. The silence of the monastery is not just the absence of television or the decision not to speak between certain hours. It is a method of being, a necessary part of the monk's life which also became a necessary part of mine. Modern men and women,

said Thomas Merton, have 'chickened out' on silence. Saint
Benedict saw silence as a virtue and devoted one chapter
of his Rule to its importance. Silence is among his list of
'tools of good works'; the monk, he writes, should try 'not
to love too much talking'. This, along with other ideas, he
calls the tools of the spiritual craft. I like his description of
monastic life as a craft. It has an apprenticeship and rules.
The notion of a craft makes the idea seem earthed, far from
those pious clouds with which the mention of a monastery
is sometimes surrounded.

I talked once with Father Columban in Mount Melleray
about the decrease in the number of monks. We went for a
walk outside the monastery on a damp afternoon, turning
at the monastery gate in the direction of Newcastle village.
This road is much different to the road from Cappoquin.

Narrow and rough in places, it was padded with animal
droppings. Sheep nudged grass near the ditches. The
landscape became more bleak as the road climbed, level
fields giving way to the rough rock that characterises so
much of that countryside.

Columban had served a term as novice master and he
told me that while fewer men entered the monastery, there
were many who applied. Most were turned down. For
some, the exercise was a passing phase characterised by a
momentary glow of interest. For others, it was a sign of
longing for solutions that would eventually be found in
some other way, or never found at all. For a handful, the
application was a strategy of mental instability. One man,
for example, said when applying that he was a friend of
one of the women in the television series *Charlie's Angels*,
and that this was a sign of his suitability for monastic life.
Of the others, a small number are taken in as novices.
Some are highly educated and most have spent a few years
living ordinary lives. Those who are accepted are not naïve.
Monastic life is difficult and those who are unsuited to it
soon realise that their place is elsewhere.

I have seen the novices in the choir, distinctive in their
white habits and with their full heads of hair set among

rows of bald or shaved, bowed heads. One novice told me that he found it hard to give up smoking. Eventually he left the monastery and, when I met him long afterwards, he said that he had found the monotony unbearable. He could put up with it no longer. Over the years, I have noticed a number of novices come and go in this way.

It can be hard to explain why so many wish to become contemplative monks or nuns. Equally, I find it hard to express my own attraction to the contemplative aspects of religious life. I think the monastery is a metaphor for what religious feeling has become for me in a new, fuller way. As with the day-to-day life, there is a wordless quality to it. While monasticism is obviously a religious quest, it has facets that are attractive and comprehensible to others, like myself, whose religious life is either confused or not at all connected to a monastic structure. Columban felt that such reasons were, in part, explanations for the fall-off in numbers. Aspects of monastic life were met by other lifestyles. He felt that hippies, for example, might fit such a category while there are others for whom an interest in, say, Zen Buddhism meets this need.

Hearing this, I was reminded of a speech Thomas Merton made in Calcutta just weeks before he died in 1968. He made statements which I have often considered and that explain part of my own attraction to Mount Melleray and to those for whom silence, simplicity and solitude is a necessary calling. He said: 'In speaking for monks I am really speaking for a very strange kind of person, a marginal person, because the monk in the modern world is no longer an established person with an established place in society. . . .Thus I find myself representing perhaps hippies among you, poets, people of this kind who are seeking in all sorts of ways and have no established status whatever. . . . Are monks and hippies and poets relevant? No, we are deliberately irrelevant. We live with an ingrained irrelevance which is proper to every human being.'

Father Columban told me that the monk's life demands physical and mental fitness, and it is not for escapists. I have heard from him and from others that monasteries are poor escape hatches, for eventually one is forced to meet oneself in darkness and silence, and that can be an unpleasant experience. The early monks lived in the desert, and the desert remains a potent symbol of deliberate withdrawal. Others, who see the world as a desert and the monastery as a romantic oasis, might well find that the desert was not all around them but within them. In what Pascal called the eternal silence of those infinite spaces, terror must surely follow. It is those who come to grips with that arid interior landscape who remain as monks or grow in a pilgrim search. They remain marginal and outside the norm — silent; as diminutive in their ambition as prayers whispered against the blackest of nightskies.

My interest in monasticism and my experience of places like Saint Gervais grew with the years and it became a rich source of ideas, poetry and confidence. There is a monk in everyone: solitary, silent, faced with questions of belief and eternity, and with the need to know God. The monk is the other side of our nature and, for those who live in Mount Melleray and elsewhere, it is the whole of it. I traced echoes of monasticism in many people whose work and example served as reflections of this same spirit that I recognised in myself. I have mentioned some of these: Eric Gill, for example, whose complicated life included an attempt to set up an artistic community which tried to combine the life of artists with religious belief and the routine of monasticism. Ludwig Wittgenstein's life seemed religious in its questing and in its honesty and intensity. I sensed it strongly in the televised pictures of the Dalai Lama, and especially in his terrific laughter.

It came across in the writings of the seventeenth-century Japanese poet, Basho, whose works are a mixture of prose and poems as he recounts his journeys across Japan. Basho's solitude and work became one. He lived as a hermit in a small house on the edge of Tokyo in 1693. I connected this house with an imaginary ninth-century cell or hut inhabited by an Irish monk on the coast. In the shattered abbey at Timoleague in County Cork, I walked among the walls and thought of Basho visiting a ruined Japanese temple. I felt again that monastic connection between temperaments from different cultures, between the ruined shrine in Japan and the ruined abbey in County Cork, and between both of them and Melleray.

One evening in Timoleague Abbey, I watched the moon and thought of how it was the same moon that Basho saw and of which he had written in small, wonderful poems. Like Thérèse of Lisieux, Basho knew the miracle of small, ordinary tasks and things — the strands of his mother's hair, the sight of a horse on a snow-filled morning. His work is as much an attitude or meditation as a collection of words, as much a spiritual perception as a physical one. As with Irish monks, the idea of pilgrimage was important to Basho. This, in turn, made him important to me.

I found elements of this search in other groups. I was impressed most of all by the Shakers, a celibate Protestant monastic group that is now almost extinct. As in a few early English monasteries, the Shakers included men and women and each lived in separate sections within the same geographical area. The American Shakers became famous for their furniture and buildings, and in the clear, simple lines of those structures I sensed the way an exterior object — a table, a recipe, a poem, a jug — becomes a reflection of an interior life. Labour and attitude were one; a direct line could be traced from, say, a life of prayer to a pot or perfectly formed box.

Where the Benedictines used the phrase *Ora et Labora* (Prayer and Work), the Shakers said 'Hands to work and minds to God'. As monks stand still or walk in silence before Mass or Office, the Shakers sat in silent prayer. In a way, the two monastic groups came together in South Union, Kentucky, where a Benedictine priory was founded in 1949 on a Shaker site. The monks moved into the old buildings. The Shaker kitchen became a Benedictine refectory.

I learned a lot from each of these individuals and groups. My understanding of them was in direct descent from my visit to Mount Melleray in 1984 and it is a continuing discovery, a pilgrimage along a path that, like Basho's road to the far north of Japan, leads to a greater unity between what I am and what I do. Taken together, these places and lives form a kind of melody. When I am properly in tune with it, I know, with Julian of Norwich, that all manner of thing shall be well.

Acknowledgements

This is a short book but, for many reasons, it was difficult to write. I am grateful to those who helped me along the way. They included the abbot and monks of Mount Melleray, especially Kevin Fogarty and Cornelius Justice. In Paris, the monks and nuns of *Les Fraternites Monastiques de Jerusalem* were welcoming and inspirational. Marie-Humbert Kennedy OP directed me towards this modern monastic order at a pivotal point. Dermot Bolger and Antony Farrell made useful comments on the manuscript at an early stage. Dermot Keogh, Mary Horan, Ken Thompson and Tina Neylon offered no end of encouragement; Dermot Keogh, in particular, made some important suggestions. In 1985, the late Liam Miller encouraged the idea of such a book. John Wilkins, editor of *The Tablet*, offered a remarkable forum as I worked out some of my ideas. Ciarain O Sabhaois, editor of the Cistercian journal *Hallel*, has been equally supportive, as have been the editors of *The Aisling*. Patricia M. Hodges, Manuscripts and Archives Supervisor, Western Kentucky University, gave me access to the writings of Thomas Whitaker, a monk whose work on the Shakers and the Benedictines mapped a territory with which I felt uncannily familiar. Gemma McCrohan and the crew of *Would You Believe* on RTE television helped me to focus on a subject that sometimes seems to defy language. Andrew Warr, at Dzogchen Beara, patiently answered my questions on Buddhism. My agent, Jonathan Williams, proved once again that his editing skills are unsurpassable.

Books, for writers, become obsessions; Trish Edelstein lived with this particular obsession and offered support and discussion. To her, and to Merlin, Owen, Gavin and Niamh, I am deeply grateful.

Seán Dunne
Cork, August 1994